PROACTIVE
CUSTOMER
SERVICE

PROACTIVE
CUSTOMER
SERVICE

*Transforming Your
Customer Service Department
Into a Profit Center*

Charles D. Brennan, Jr.

AMACOM
American Management Association

New York • Atlanta • Boston • Chicago • Kansas City • San Francisco • Washington, D.C.
Brussels • Mexico City • Tokyo • Toronto

This publication is designed to provide accurate and authoritative
information in regard to the subject matter covered. It is sold with
the understanding that the publisher is not engaged in rendering
legal, accounting, or other professional service. If legal advice or
other expert assistance is required, the services of a competent
professional person should be sought.

Library of Congress Cataloging-in-Publication Data

Brennan, Charles D.
     Proactive customer service : transforming your customer service
department into a profit center / Charles D. Brennan, Jr.
       p.   cm.
   Includes index.
   ISBN 0-8144-0372-7
   1. Customer services—Management.   I. Title.
   HF5415.5.B737   1997
   658.8'12—dc21   97–21788
                                           CIP

Printing number

10 9 8 7 6 5 4 3 2 1

To **Annette,** my partner and best friend,

and

to my family: **Amanda, Daniel,** and **Christina,**

for your love.

Thank you

for your confidence and encouragement at the beginning;

for your support in providing me with the opportunity to make my ideas and career a reality;

and for the strength and love of our family, which makes it all worthwhile.

Contents

Acknowledgments

Special thanks go to Susan Gurevitz, for her ability to transform my thoughts and explain my concepts, which helped to provide the reader with an easy-to-use book for assistance in professional development. I express my appreciation for her dedication to this project and recognition of her expertise for communicating and capturing the issues and ideas necessary for making this book an effective learning tool and guide.

I would like to express my sincere thanks for the help and input received from:

Bill Skinner
Fred Tunney
Andrew Trackman
Lars Mawn
Robert Burton
Gary Moore
Bernie Coley

Your knowledge and experience of the marketplace was invaluable in the development of my book. Thanks for your time and effort in producing the information necessary to enable this book to address and provide real world, day-to-day customer service issues. Also, special thanks to your support of our concepts throughout the years, and enabling us to work with your professionals.

PROACTIVE CUSTOMER SERVICE

1

"Believe Me—It Can Be Done"

New Initiatives for CSRs

Customer service. We hear about it all the time. People want good customer service. Companies pride themselves on their excellent customer service. And, yes, your customers demand efficient customer service. In theory, if we improve our company's customer service, that will help increase sales. But let's face it. Within the past decade most successful companies have climbed that customer service mountain and, with each crevice, added all kinds of helpful gear as climbing aids. As I talk with sales training executives from companies all over the country, I hear all sorts of comments and complaints about how improving customer service has become, quite frankly, a real pain. As Bill Skinner, head of sales training at one of America's largest pharmaceutical companies, dryly puts it, "In corporate America, we seem to succumb to fads, like 'teaming' and 'empowerment.' "

But, I assure you, teaching what we call "advanced consultative selling skills" to your customer service representatives is not just another corporate fad. The need to convert your CSRs from their traditional reactive roles to a proactive inside sales force is very real. In fact, it's so real that I believe adding CSRs to the company's sales team is one of the few options still available for boosting the bottom line. If, instead of a book on customer service selling, I were to write my own version of Alvin

Toffler's *Future Shock*, this is what I'd confidently predict: Within the next decade the classic sales force, which may number in the hundreds, will be cut in half, while the number of CSRs will double. And I didn't come to this conclusion after a long night of imbibing with friends.

What? You say your CSRs don't want to adopt a proactive role? Have you asked them? You'd be amazed at how much CSRs enjoy taking a active position and meeting the challenge that accompanies it once they feel confident because they've learned the steps of asking the right kinds of questions, gathering selected information, and guiding the customer along toward the close.

As I said earlier, sales executives at a variety of companies recognize the growing marketplace demands for enhancing the questioning and listening skills of its CSR department so that it can evolve into an efficient inside sales force and augment the activities of outside salespeople. The executives from organizations such as the national accounting firm of Deloitte & Touche, the U.S. Postal Service, MCI Communications, Polaroid, Wyeth-Ayerst, and Softmart all acknowledge the necessity of altering their sales approach in order to beat out the competition. As the sales training manager at MCI points out, "Our CSRs and sales team work together to interpret the customer's needs." Most corporate comments, as you will read later on, sing a similar tune, with some variation on the lyrics.

How's your ear for music? Be honest with yourself. Aren't you just a tad worried whether you'll be able to maintain your sales pace over the next few years? What are you going to recommend to your superiors in your long-range plan? Maybe your annual sales increases are getting leaner and leaner, and you've already shifted territories and taken other restructuring steps. Now's the time to take a second look at your customer service representatives—your budding inside sales team. Over the years, CSRs have taken on some additional duties, but they've always fallen under the category of "reactive," responding to a customer's request for help or information. Now's the time to change that.

To illustrate the alternatives, let's look at the CSR's changing role as a continuum, running from one to ten, with one serving as the most basic customer service reactive function, and ten represented by a CSR who's completely taken on the proactive role as an inside salesperson. At the first level, we have the most basic customer service, such as a bank teller. The key phrase that describes the reactive mode is "How can I help you?" Here's a common scenario. Typically, the teller just takes your deposits and completes your withdrawals. Selling information is relegated to point-of-purchase brochures sitting at the teller windows. More recently, at some more forward-thinking banks, at the end of the transaction the teller might also tell you about a new service, and ask you if you'd like more information on it. If so, you're referred to one of the loan reps. That's where the teller's role stops. There's a hint of a proactive move here, but the teller is still basically a reactive employee.

Let's move up the continuum now to levels three and four, to a customer service rep who acts as a troubleshooter. It's still the reactive "How can I help you" mode, but it also tosses in an element of "Do you know we're running a special on nonelectronic office supplies?" Even though the CSR is introducing a touch of "proactiveness," it's still the more traditional CSR role. Consider the following example. You call the customer service rep at the department store where you bought your VCR about two years ago. Much to your chagrin, the VCR is suddenly not working properly, and it chewed up your favorite tape of "Gone With the Wind." The store customer rep is very apologetic, and notes that you had purchased the service contract, so there will be no charge for the repair. In addition, they will also replace your copy of "Gone With the Wind." Remember, service contracts were the customer service "improvement" introduced in the 1980s. Even though they cost extra, they're portrayed as a special favor from the retailer. Granted, they're only an expensive insurance policy—until you need them, of course. Oh yes. The rep mentions that the store is having a special on big-screen TV sets, and according to her records, you last bought a TV eight years ago, so you might be ready for a new one. There's her pitch, but unless you're truly in the market for a new TV, you don't bite.

The CSR Evolution Continuum

Now that we've visited the first, third, and fourth levels of our CSR evolution continuum, we'll jump to higher levels, say six, seven, and eight. While the lower levels represent consumer operations, we now move into business-to-business circumstances. At these levels, our CSRs are seeking customer sales opportunities in a more aggressive active manner, so they require a whole new group of skills related to questioning, listening, determining their objectives, and otherwise pursuing the client. For example, the CSR at Painless Medical Products receives a phone call from a regular customer, a purchasing manager for a chain of nursing homes, who thinks he's placing his regular order. The CSR knows that her company is trying to sell a new line of rubberized sheets and pillow cases. So the CSR begins asking probing questions, looking for additional pieces of information about the new markets into which the customer is moving, according to a recent newspaper article, and that the competition may not know about. Through a series of multilayered probing questions, she learns that the nursing home chain is not terribly happy with its current rubber sheets because they cause the patients to sweat profusely. She also learns who the decision makers are at the company and convinces her contact to put her in touch with one of them.

This example tells you that we've catapulted beyond the traditional CSR role and made dramatic progress toward our goal. At the final level, CSRs are completely converted into their new, active position with your company and are so adept that they can be assigned small and medium-size accounts because they know how to resolve customer objections, present their solutions, and gain customer commitment. They've also uncovered new decision makers, furthering the account penetration. And they have progressed toward becoming what I call "advanced consultative service representatives," or ACSRs. They no longer are simply customer service reps.

I hope this illustration of the continuum has painted a picture of your CSRs' potential. Here's a ready resource that, through a series of new skills, can ultimately boost your sales, and, I don't mind saying, make you look like a hero in the process. Through the series of instructions, exercises, company stories, and illustrations contained in this book, CSRs will learn how to generate new business opportunities by asking the right questions, engaging the customer in dialogue, applying advanced listening skills, and leveraging existing relationships. This process has been geared toward recognizing that the customer is important. And that's the key.

Why Do You Need to Change the CSR's Role?

Why is this advanced consultative selling process for CSRs necessary? No matter how large or small your company is or what product or service it sells, no matter what approach your company has used or is now considering, the goal is still the same—to keep the customer happy so that he continues to buy your wares. But, as I said earlier with my Toffler hat on, once again our business environment is changing. Just a few years ago companies were falling all over themselves to find the newest management technique that would improve the bottom line. Some jumped into total quality management (TQM), while others adopted some other variation on the theme of team building. Even though some of these techniques may have worked, and many companies have successfully adopted them, we've still bogged down in a reactive mode.

The Tough Competitive Environment

Pay closer attention to your competitive environment. "How may I help you" is no longer good enough to get a jump on the competition. Your business is moving at a much faster pace, and companies have downsized, reengineered, gotten lean and mean, what have you. No industry is immune from the fierce competition that has continued to grow as companies realign, reconfigure, and merge resources. Parity reigns within most markets. As the senior training adviser at a *Fortune* 100 international commodity-selling company told me, the selling environment and pace have changed dramatically, thanks, in part, to technology, along with the need to keep just one step ahead of the other guy.

"It used to be that, whatever people wanted, if you had the materials available you could simply sell them. Price or service didn't matter. But now the pace has picked up tremendously, and if a customer has a request, they want a response the same day," he says. At the same time, the buying population doesn't have as much time to spend with a traditional salesperson anymore. Just look at your own in-box and the pile of phone messages on your desk. "The products we sell don't differ all that much from the competition, so the issue has become how easy it is for people to do business with you," points out this senior training adviser. He believes the role of a salesperson is to assist the buyer, rather than just sell the buyer. "And that's what customer service has got to be," he adds.

I couldn't agree with him more. If you don't go after every customer with even more gusto and aggressiveness than your competition can muster, you're going to be left in your competitor's dust. It may be tough to envision your CSRs as part of the selling team, as ACSRs, but consider, for example, the accounting industry. Here we have a group of people who were originally trained to work with numbers, balance sheets, and accounting methodology. These accounting firm partners and partner "wanna-bes" have gradually realized that they also have to be salespeople and generate new business. A new client doesn't just come walking in the door anymore, she has to be won. That's why we've seen such a major contraction in that industry over the past decade. The same can be said for the legal industry, where law firms have merged or simply shut down because they didn't have enough "rainmakers"—people who can generate new business.

Leaner, Pared-Down Workforces

Take a lesson from the accounting and legal industries, and arm yourself with every piece of customer-serving and customer-saving ammunition at your disposal—your CSRs. "You've got to become a futurist and anticipate what skills your people will need," the senior training adviser told me.

But for many companies that's tough to do, because during the reengineering process we've also reduced our sales forces. Salespeople are spread thinner, with larger territories to cover. As the sales reps generate new customers, it's physically impossible for them to make regular sales calls to every customer on their books. Besides, we all know how costly a sales call can be. At the same time, information is driving sales these days. As Fred Tunney, the sales training manager at Polaroid, told me, "In all of our eight customer surveys ten years ago, customers wanted human contact, but not anymore. They just want the information." That applies to larger customers as well as to Polaroid's smaller dealers, who just don't have the time to meet face to face with sales reps anymore.

Ideal Positioning

Too many of us are still viewing customer service representatives in the same way we always have. CSRs have been trained to ask the calling customer what the problem is, solve the problem, and get back to the customer with a solution maybe the next day or the day after. Perhaps they're rewarded with merit raises, or maybe a bonus tossed in here and there. Sound familiar?

Here's a key point to remember. What have we been overlooking here in our zeal to become more productive and improve the corporate bottom line? Who probably has more regular contact with your customers than your CSRs? Perhaps you've got an entire department whose only responsibility is to handle customer complaints, problems, and questions. Take a second look at it. You're staring at a ready resource that is expected only to maintain and retain customer relationships and that simply functions in a reactive mode. But is there more these CSRs can do to contribute to the company's bottom line? In a word, certainly. I can prove it, as can the various sales managers and trainers who will tell their stories throughout this book.

As these corporate execs have experienced, instead of using the CSRs as reactive people, you can refocus their efforts and view them as an inside sales team that can function as an adjunct to your outside sales force. They can become an active part of the sales process. Consider the experiences of the sales training executive of another major international corporation.

"Our customer service department used to be what a traditional order entry department was. But gradually, we realized that, besides taking orders, these people could function as an inside sales force because they talk to the customers on a daily basis and can identify a customer's problem. Even though no one had really recognized their importance before, they have now become part of the sales process because we've figured out how to use the information they can generate," he says. "These people have had sales as well as product training to understand the company's product line. In many cases the CSRs go out on sales calls with the salespeople so they can meet the customers in person.

"There's a big difference between what our CSRs did ten years ago and what they do today," the sales training exec continues. "Before, they were regarded just like clerks or order takers. That's not the case today."

Clearly, this company has rewritten the CSRs' job description and given them a new direction, responsibility, and role in the company. CSRs have been trained to generate new sales and to identify opportunities for cross-selling that they may either handle themselves or hand over to a member of the sales team. But bear in mind that this company has realized how to capitalize on a resource through a gradual process. Your company may not have several years to gradually turn your CSRs into inside sales associates.

Making the Transition

So what do you do? Adopting this approach may require some alterations in your sales culture and CSR reward system. The culture change could be as dramatic as that at Polaroid, when it completely restructured its sales operation and moved all its CSR-type people into one facility, with the responsibility of handling the smaller customers. Or you can begin by shifting your view of CSRs and their view of themselves. The criteria that used to dictate their reward system are now a prerequisite for their new responsibilities. Sure, you may offer incentives, but you're also officially recognizing their existing skills and boosting their self-confidence in the importance of their current position. For example, when a copy machine technician is asked to also sell paper and cartridges and to discuss the new leasing rates in a cross-selling effort, he can derive satisfaction from the confidence you've displayed in him. And he can understand how his existing skills (his relationship with the customer) can be translated into another kind of relationship.

Although initially your CSRs might feel apprehension and even fear about their new responsibilities, they don't have to jump in the pool without any waterwings. The techniques introduced in this book were originally designed for outside salespeople, and can be easily applied and taught to these newly discovered inside salespeople. This process can instruct CSRs to differentiate your product while avoiding the tired traditional sales approach—what I like to call the "would you like fries with your burger" strategy. That approach is really a dinosaur, just like that 286 or 386 computer that's still sitting on your desk. Instead, this approach is more like the most advanced Pentium MMX computer chip. Among other strategies, your CSRs will learn how to ask a series of probing questions to gather information on the customer's needs—a crucial element for knowing when it's time to close the sales. In short, these people can help boost your sales efforts and take advantage of the relationships they've built with customers. You're not starting from scratch but simply introducing them to some new challenges and responsibilities.

In the next few chapters I discuss what issues CSRs encounter and how they can handle them by learning a new art of questioning customers about their needs. I begin by discussing how various company salespeople have restructured and retrained their CSRs to be productive members of their company's sales team. As Alvin Toffler would say, "The future is now."

2

"But I Like My Job the Way It Is"

New Role for CSRs

We all like to feel comfortable, whether we're sinking down into a favorite overstuffed chair to watch a football game on TV or socializing with friends who share our enthusiasm for golf. That's comfort. But what happens when that overstuffed chair just doesn't fit with the other new furniture, or your favorite golfing buddies move away? Those situations signal change, and we all know that change is a tough topic—just to address, let alone initiate. It's even tougher in the business world, where people feel comfortable with their jobs, knowing the routine and their bosses' expectations. Makes you nervous just thinking about it, right?

But during the past decade few companies have been immune from some sort of reorganization, buyouts, spin-offs, or downsizing—ugh, change. Your competitor's business is shifting, and so is yours, and if your company is going to compete effectively, it's going to have to alter the roles of different departments. This can be frightening, intimidating, and threatening, especially if the change is an unknown entity. Ask anyone who's gone through it. The trick, of course, is to view change as a challenge, an opportunity to do something a bit differently and maybe even to learn to enjoy it. And it's up to you, and upper management, to present it that way. After all, these days change has become a constant, but it's traumatic and difficult only if you're unprepared for it. In this chapter we look at how some major companies have overcome obstacles to change and revised the role of their traditional customer service reps from a reactive, "can I help you" operation into a more active sales mode through specialized sales training and support.

The Changing Role of the CSR

Customer service representatives have typically been hired simply to respond to customer queries—a comfortable role. But because CSRs have built up friendly relationships with customers over the years, it's natural to begin viewing them as an inside sales force, giving them new responsibilities for selling your products and services. Certainly, presenting CSRs with a new set of expectations is not a simple task, primarily because CSRs lack the confidence to become a member of the company's sales team. If they wanted to be in sales, that's where they'd be.

Let me give you two typical phone dialogues. One illustrates a typical conversation with a CSR who hasn't had any sales training; the second is a dialogue initiated by a CSR who has undergone training as an inside sales rep.

Dialogue 1: Before Training

[*The customer, Bob Smith, calls the CSR because he's having trouble with his software.*]

CSR: Did you check to see that it's properly installed?
Bob: Yes, that seems OK, but I just can't get my Internet connection to work right.
CSR: Is your system designed to run this software? Is your phone system adequate?
Bob: Yes, your technician told me I shouldn't have any problems, even though I have an older system.
CSR: It could be your phone system. Have you spoken with the phone company?
Bob: No, should I?
CSR: Not necessarily. We are now offering a phone plan that would

cost you an extra $5 a month, and I see by our records that you're spending $20 a month now for the phone company hookup. So you'd be saving yourself $15 a month, or nearly $200 a year.

Bob: And that would work on my system?

CSR: Absolutely. This gives you a dedicated phone line, so there shouldn't be any interference or problem with your Internet connection.

Bob: That's great. Sign me up!

CSR: Are you satisfied with this phone call?

Bob: Certainly. Thank you.

CSR: Thank you, Bob, and please call again if we can help you with something.

[*The CSR is pleased because she closed the sale, and the customer is happy.*]

Dialogue 2: After Training

[*The customer, Bob Smith, calls with a problem involving his phone system.*]

CSR: Bob, I see from our records that you are signed up for our new calling plan. Can you describe your calling patterns and tell me how they've evolved over the past, say, two years or so? (*Here, you're looking for new opportunities and gaining information.*)

Bob: Well, I have a new partner, and we've divided up the duties more, so I'm doing a lot more traveling. I guess that means I'm making more long distance phone calls.

CSR: Gosh, that can be costly, huh?

Bob: Yes, it is. I really hate looking at the phone bills every month.

CSR: Tell me, when you're traveling, is it sometimes tough to get to a phone, especially if you want to call home late at night?

Bob: Right. You know the hotels charge an extra fee for making a call, so I try to avoid the room phones because I really disagree with that policy.

CSR: I know what you mean. How about if you had your own 800 number? It's reasonably priced, especially compared to your current long distance phone bills, and it also allows you to bypass those access fees charged by the hotels.

Bob: No kidding. And an 800 number would save me money?

CSR: On the basis of your current billing records, I estimate you could save as much as 15 percent a month, depending on your usage.

Bob: That sounds like exactly what I need.

CSR: Tell me something else. Because you travel so much, it seems to me that a cellular phone could come in really handy. And we currently have a special offer on a top-of-the-line cellular phone.

Bob: I've always wanted a cellular phone, but, to be honest, they've seemed kind of complicated to me.

CSR: I know what you mean. A lot of people have had that problem over the years with some of the earlier models, but the one we're offering with this special package is really easy to use. I attended a demonstration on it just today. (*countering his objections*)

Bob: That sounds really good, too.

CSR: Tell me, does your partner have a cellular phone?

Bob: No, but this sounds like a good idea for him, too.

CSR: Do you both work out of the same office?

Bob: No, he works out of our Yardley office in Bucks County.

CSR: Isn't that a toll call?

Bob: It sure is, and there's no way around it, but that location is ideal for serving our New Jersey and New York clients.

CSR: I understand. That must be very frustrating. But the 800 number I mentioned earlier would eliminate those long-distance phone charges.

Bob: Really? That would be terrific.

CSR: Tell me, Bob, do you make the buying decisions for your operation, or does your partner?

Bob: My partner, Jim Jolly, makes these kinds of decisions. And I'd really like to take you up on the 800 phone number and those cellular phones. Here's Jim's phone number, 610-449-6110.

CSR: Will you be speaking with him soon so that he'll know to expect my phone call?

Bob: Yes, in fact he's on his way here for a meeting right now. I'll tell him about our conversation.

CSR: Are you going to recommend my suggestions to him?

Bob: Absolutely.

CSR: So when would be a good time for me to contact him today?

Bob: Since he's going to be here all afternoon, why not call back at about 2:00 P.M.? Will you be able to give him some exact numbers on what the 800 number and cell phones will cost us?

CSR: Certainly, I will work out all the numbers for you before I call back later.

Aside from the length of the two conversations, it should be obvious how much more information the CSR gleaned using the second script, and how the CSR countered Bob's concerns about cellular phones. She also got Bob to explain his needs, identify the decision maker, and offer to recommend her products, as well as to give a commitment to change. These are elements that we look for in a CSR trained in advanced consultative selling. In the first dialogue, the CSR simply offered the product without gaining any additional information about the customer to see whether Bob might be ripe for other services. The point was to be quick and to try to keep the customer happy. Sure, she sold Bob a new phone service, but she never really got a commitment to change from Bob. And there was little relationship building, so what's to stop him from changing his mind if another phone service salesperson calls him later that same day?

A New Way of Doing Business

In the past, the primary job descriptions for pure customer sales reps have been pretty standard, with the emphasis on speed at handling calls. The objective was, and in many cases still is, to not keep a customer waiting on the phone for long. A customer's time is valuable, and if she can't get through to your company, she just might hang up and call a competitor. For example, consider one aspect of the customer service operation that I recently observed at one of the country's most respected investment management companies. The company has a Times Square–type of rolling message screen on the wall, as you might expect, but it isn't there to report the latest numbers from Wall Street. Instead, it's there to keep track of how many customers are calling, how many are waiting, and how many are currently being helped. That's the classic definition of customer service. But suppose this company wants to move its CSRs into the proactive role of selling, perhaps, some mutual funds. That operations room might run this way: At the front of the room a red light is blinking, indicating that a customer is on hold. CSR#1 has to quickly hang up on the current phone call and pick up the blinking one because that's one of the criteria for her performance. But now CSR#1 is operating in a proactive mode, and she needs to build a relationship with her current phone customer, so the red light may have to blink just a bit longer while she asks questions and furthers the relationship with her current call. Obviously, this requires a longer conversation with her first phone call, but just by a few minutes.

Let's discuss this "blinking light" dilemma. Certainly, it presents a cultural and systematic problem. How can she talk to the customer, meet her performance criteria, and still uncover new opportunities while that infernal light is blinking? You see, simply offering quick customer service might not be enough. "It's almost as naive as the salesperson who believes that if I can't answer your question I'll find out and let you know. That's become so stereotypical of customer service that it's no longer a service," points out Bill Skinner at Wyeth. Remember, CSRs are a rich company resource that can affect the bottom line. They can help you generate and seek out new business opportunities. But they can't perform well in a vacuum. It's a systematic problem that management has to view realistically. If the first change is shifting your CSRs into a sales force, the next change has got to be a restructuring that allows the CSRs to do their jobs, even if the red light is blinking. As an example, let's look at how a major corporate reseller of Microsoft products introduced change to his customer service department and what his experiences have been.

Bob Burton, vice president of sales and marketing at Softmart Corp., restructured his sales department several years ago. He acknowledges that attacking any other challenge might have been easier. "Customer service used to be under operations, but in the reorganization we brought it under sales and combined telemarketing and customer service representatives into teams," he explains. "Customer service used to just be a department for placing orders and asking questions. It was totally disconnected from the sales department."

Then, enter the reorganization. To Burton and Ron Sullivan (VP of Operations), teaming up customer service and telemarketing made a whole lot of sense, but his CSRs didn't look at it that way. "The customer service people didn't like to be associated with those despicable salespeople," he recalls with a chuckle. The new roles were introduced by telemarketing managers and customer service managers, and some of the customer service managers actually became sales managers.

"We did go through a gradual process of convincing the CSRs that they could do this and emphasizing that for a customer to order another product is not an ugly sales thing but really a customer service," Burton says. To illustrate how making a sales recommendation over the phone would make their jobs easier, he used the example of a customer buying a word processor as well as the associated products. "We told them, 'I'm doing a disservice to my customer if I don't recommend it.'" Still, his CSRs saw their new sales roles as "repulsive," especially telling customers about some special offers. "They just didn't see that as their responsibility."

Let me add my two cents' worth here. What CSRs need to understand is that customers trust them because they have helped them in the past. They've gone beyond that initial "sales thing" of establishing a relationship with the customer. They're really in the best position to sell those customers additional products. Now back to Burton's story.

"We integrated [the new approach] over the years, and our customer service people now see themselves as performing their function as a customer service and not as sales. But it was a good six months before our people felt comfortable being 'proactive,'" he says. Prior to the restructuring, CSRs underwent only a day or two of job training. Today, new CSRs go through a full three weeks of training in technology as well as role playing. "We've continually expanded [our training program]," Burton says. In fact, today the customer service department reports to the sales manager. Not all the CSRs made the transition successfully, but the department boasts an inside team of 100 people.

MCI, one of the largest and fastest growing telecommunications companies in the world, has a similar story to tell, but it has taken the teaming of customer service and sales a step further.

Marketing manager Andrew Trackman explains that the company has incorporated technology into the workplace, empowering its business sales and service employees with information at their fingertips that can be readily shared with customers and with each other. Using laptop computers and intranet technology, both sales and service professionals have access to the same information, enabling either rep to research, retrieve, and immediately deliver products and account information to their customers.

This approach to "virtual teaming" allows sales and service to work in tandem—supporting each other's traditional roles—to best support a customer's day-to-day account requirements. "They go on sales calls together so they can both interpret the customer's needs. They both hear the same story." Trackman also views the CSR role as a means of building multiple relationships with a customer, and gaining multilevel penetration within an account. "For example, the sales rep might work with the CFO, and the customer service rep might work with accounts receivable or the MIS department. In every scenario, we are providing a highly responsive, team approach to serving the customer."

This approach not only helps MCI generate new business opportunities but also offers their salespeople more flexibility to meet their target goals. "Because our customer service reps are not viewed as the traditional salesperson, the customer is much more receptive, especially to cross-selling," he says. "It's like the icing on the cake."

Of course, not all of the customer service reps happened to like that flavor of icing. "As with all change, initially we encountered a bit of resistance," Trackman acknowledges. "The sales reps were a bit threatened, and the customer service reps felt they were stepping out of their comfort zone. The customer service reps were not used to doing sales calls."

To overcome these obstacles, MCI trained the sales reps to make the initial sale and initiate the relationship with a customer, while moving the CSRs into a new role they call strategic service reps. Each team member's role is distinct. For example, the strategic sales representative's job is more warm and fuzzy; this person is expected to do the homework on the company before the sales call. "It's a challenge, but it keeps our sales reps out in the field where they belong and keeps our strategic sales reps up with our new products."

That's a particularly important point. Almost any business forecast you read predicts continuing change in how business is conducted, whether it's increasing use of the Internet or another kind of communication device that hasn't even been invented yet. In fact, MCI itself predicts that 50 percent of its profits in the year 2000 will come from business lines that the company is not even selling today.

The point I've tried to illustrate here is that we're actually looking at three levels of change: Management has to recognize the need for a restructuring change to support the CSRs' efforts; CSRs need to learn how to accept and execute the changes in their job; and CSRs want to encourage the customer to acknowledge the need for change.

The tried-and-true traditions of selling your products and services need to be reviewed and revised just to keep up with the competition, let alone just ahead of it. I'm not saying that you have to institute your corporate changes exactly as Softmart and MCI did. Don't be afraid to be creative in instituting your own process and performance criteria based on your own particular circumstances. Frankly, your CSRs may be your hardest sell, but accepting change in their duties is just as vital to them as convincing a customer to acknowledge the need for change.

I believe that it's important for CSRs to experience change in their job responsibilities so that they can better understand how to convince the customer about the need for change. That firsthand experience can be crucial seasoning for the training process. Once the CSRs are baked and out of the training oven, you'll have produced an entree that would make Martha Stewart proud. I call this entree "advanced consultative service representatives," or ASCRs. Not only do the ASCRs eliminate the need to hire additional salespeople; they also add a vital ingredient to your entire selling meal. We examine these ingredients, as well as strategies, in the next few chapters. Just don't get too comfortable yet. We still have several more courses to go.

3

"Getting to Know You"

Building and Expanding Relationships

A friend of mine recently found a book, published in the 1940s, that proposes to unravel some of the mysteries of husband/wife relationships. You can probably guess at some of the advice doled out by the expert who wrote this book—mostly to the wife, of course—about how she should welcome her husband home from his hard day of work, and on and on. Obviously, this *Father Knows Best* scenario is hopelessly out of date in today's dual-working-spouses, postfeminist environment. But that was how people built and maintained important relationships fifty years ago. It was the standard of the times, and most people accepted it.

The same could probably be said for sales strategies geared towards building relationships with customers. How did our fathers and grandfathers (few moms and no grandmothers, I'm afraid) sell their products to their clients? Even just ten years ago we approached a sales call differently from the way we do today, mainly due to major changes in the business environment and increased competition. We have more sophisticated techniques and skills, to say nothing of a broader and constantly growing range of products and services. Establishing a solid relationship with the customer has always served as the foundation for building sales, just as a healthy relationship with one's spouse serves as the cornerstone for a happy marriage. The point here is that relationship building in the sales world must change along with the marketplace, just as personal relationships have changed over the decades.

What does this have to do with customer service? Simple. We've already discussed how many large and small companies have been or are in the midst of changing their customer service reps into some version of an inside sales team. CSR job descriptions have been rewritten to include generating sales, in addition to answering customers' questions and taking orders. "We call it one-stop shopping," Fred Tunney of Polaroid tells me when describing the company's fledgling Customer Care Center. But, as many sales training and marketing managers I've talked with readily admit, getting traditional CSRs up to snuff with the proper skills is not that easy. I had to chuckle when Bob Burton of Softmart (see Chapter 2) talks about having to convince former pure customer service reps that selling other products to their customers was not "repulsive." As Bob points out to his people, "to order another product is not an ugly sales thing, but really a customer service."

If we now expect our CSRs to generate sales and broaden our penetration into the client company, we need to make sure they possess the same sales skills that our senior salespeople have learned and use successfully on a daily basis. Training to be an inside sales person does, indeed, differ dramatically from traditional sales training, both in the time spent and in content. Salespeople are used to attending regular seminars on selling techniques. That's not the case with CSRs. But due to their unique position as the traditional front-line people vis-à-vis the customers, the newly charged CSRs will benefit from learning the advanced consultative sales skills that are used by their sales counterparts to manage their time, ask the right questions, and close a sale without letting the customer realize she's being engaged or sold to. In fact, I'd go so far as to say that it's mandatory for CSRs to learn advanced consultative selling skills before they attempt to sell a customer. And in case you're part of a sales team, or sales management, and have never encountered this approach before, you can learn how this system works as well. That's the reason that throughout the book I address you as well as your CSRs. So now, let's begin with sales call pacing, an initial but crucial aspect of this approach.

The Quarter-Half-Quarter Model

The guide for pacing a sales call is based on a system called the quarter-half-quarter model, which serves as a road map for this new inside sales team. The entire process hangs on this model, which is designed to teach how to pace a sale and when to apply the four phases of consultative selling (see Figure 3-1). These are:

Phase 1:	Opening
Phase 2:	Building relationships, questioning and listening, agreeing on needs and change
Phase 3:	Presenting your solution
Phase 4:	Gaining commitment to action

Figure 3-1. The quarter-half-quarter model for placing a sales call.

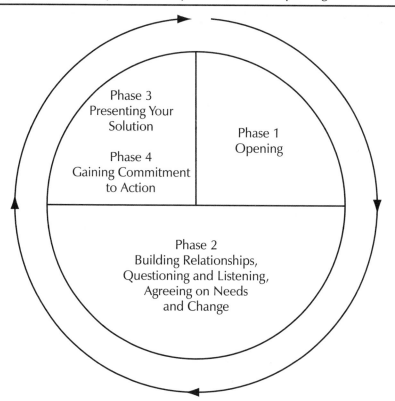

Even though this may at first seem complicated to your new sales charges, they can always keep a copy of the model on their desks, since the bulk of their customer contact is over the phone. Also, they really have an advantage over their sales rep brethren and can probably skip some aspects of Phase I (Opening) because they have already established a relationship with the customer through previous customer service contact. Let's briefly review the key elements of each phase and where and why they appear in each section of the quarter-half-quarter model.

Phase 1: Opening (Figure 3-2). There are five steps in phase 1, designed to begin building your relationship with the customer: introduction, establishing common ground, gaining interest, creating your agenda, and setting your objectives. The final two

Figure 3-2.   Phase 1: Opening.

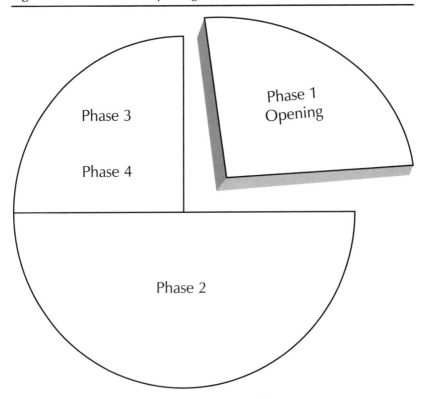

steps require you to actually plan out how you're going to approach the customer and to determine your goals.

Phase 2: Building Relationships, Questioning and Listening, Agreeing on Needs and Change (Figure 3-3). This phase is the most complicated, and, as you can see in Figure 3-3, it accounts for the "half" part of the model. It focuses on the important elements of building a relationship and establishing questioning techniques and serves as the information-gathering phase. Clearly, if this phase is not executed properly, it's impossible to move on to the next quarter and succeed.

Because of the importance of this phase, I've spent a great

Figure 3-3. Phase 2: Building relationships, questioning and listening, agreeing on needs and changes.

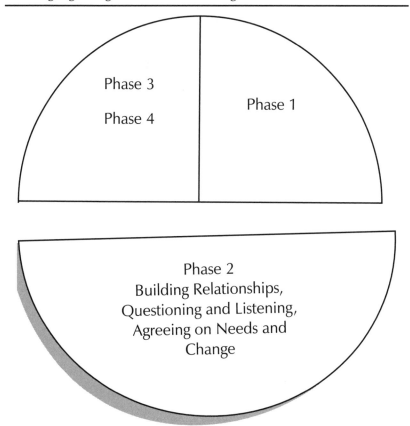

deal of time developing and refining the questioning and listening processes used in it. I've identified several kinds of questioning techniques that go beyond the usual "w" questions—who,
what, where, why, when. These new techniques fall under the
category of the multilayered probing questions (MLPQ), which I
describe in more detail in Chapter 6. By asking dialogue-probing
questions and countering questions, the CSR will be able to trace
the history of the company's sales, expand the customer's
"needs" list, identify the decision makers and the extent of their
interest, and acquire a commitment to change.

Phase 3: Presenting Your Solution (Figure 3-4). Congratulations to your CSR for moving into this phase, because that
means she has successfully accomplished the questioning, lis-

Figure 3-4.   Phase 3: Presenting your solution, and Phase 4:
Gaining commitment to action.

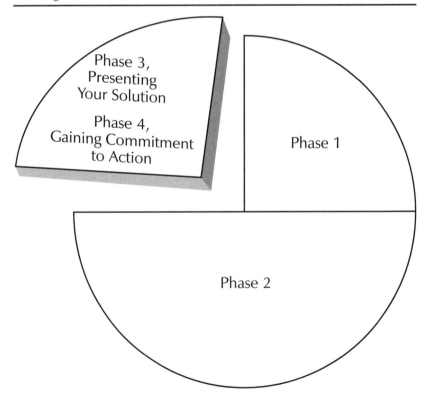

tening, and information-gathering process of the "half" portion of the model. In this final quarter, the CSR offers a solution statement and presents your product or service as the solution to the customer's needs. Following that, the CSR accepts the customer's confirmation, meaning that the customer does indeed want to buy your product or service. Your CSR has managed to pace herself and to control the conversation.

Phase 4: Gaining Commitment to Action (Figure 3-4). Eureka! The check is in the mail—really.

This quarter-half-quarter model has been intentionally designed to be flexible. It can be adapted depending on the salesperson's rapport with the customer as well as the service or product he's selling. That means that Phases 1 and 2 might be condensed because of the CSR's previous relationship with the customer or because the product is in such demand (think of Christmas 1996, when that year's most desirable toy, Tickle Me Elmo, became every parent's nightmare and every three-year-old's dream) that the CSR won't even need to apply every phase of the "half" section and will be able to move more quickly into the final commitment phase (see Figure 3-5). Bear in mind, too, that even CSRs who are new to the department are still ahead of the game because they're on the receiving end of the phone call, like a football team's wide-end receiver. The customer is calling for a specific reason—to ask a question, put in an order, or check on his credit line. The trick—and any wide-end receiver could tell you this—is for the receiver to know what to do once he catches the ball—whether literally or figuratively.

Not long ago the New York Sales and Marketing Club conducted a survey on the major reasons people make certain purchases. The most frequently cited reason for purchasing decisions was not price or value but the relationship with the individual. Let me repeat that. Relationship. In a follow-up study, a UCLA professor looked at what influences our relationships. Words accounted for 7 percent of the responses, vocal elements accounted for 38 percent, and nonverbal actions topped the list at 55 percent. Look again at the 7 percent response for words. A sales presentation is words, isn't it? Think about it. When you rely on just words, without any of the relationship-building elements, you're doomed to failure.

Figure 3-5. Condensing Phases 1 and 2 of the quarter-half-quarter model.

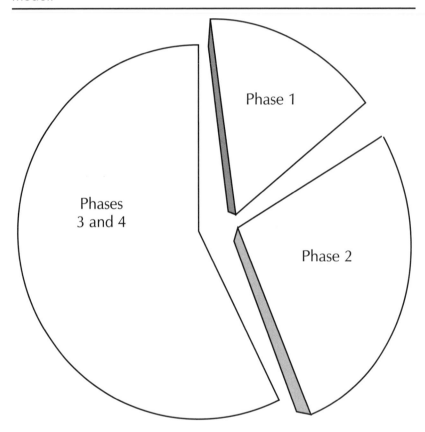

By relying upon the quarter-half-quarter model, CSRs-in-training can focus on expanding their role with the customer from merely answering questions to asking questions directly and gathering information. In other words, CSRs can redirect how the customers perceive them by adopting the stance of a consultant and steering the customer in the most desirable direction. This clearly signals a more active role for CSRs. In addition, by asking probing questions and listening carefully to the answers, CSRs position themselves as partners, rather than just salespeople. At the same time, CSRs set up the opportunity to diagnose and study the customer's needs. In short, finding out additional facts about the customer sets the stage for offering suggestions for change.

Think about the various consultants you may have worked with over the years. The good consultants really become part of your team, getting to know your particular department inside and out. Over time, you develop a trust in the consultant and may even get to the point where you forget this person is not an employee of your company. The same could be said for the budding relationship between the CSR and the customer. The CSR maintains the one-on-one relationship already established with the customer, while massaging it to offer the customer more than he's actually asking for. That's what Phase 2 of the quarter-half-quarter model is designed to do.

Let me give you another everyday example to help you understand the point. Several weeks ago, as you snuggled down in your favorite chair with a steaming cup of coffee to read the Sunday *New York Times,* you nonchalantly picked up the travel section. What a great section to browse through! Then, something caught your eye. Maybe it was an advertised trip to Puerto Rico, the Florida Keys, or even Europe. It sounded great. You showed the ad to your spouse, and you both agreed, "Let's do it. After all, we certainly owe it to ourselves. We need to get away." (Who doesn't?)

You call the travel agent first thing Monday morning. She offers to send you the brochures right away. When they arrive a couple of days later, you're excited and thrilled at the prospect of this needed trip. You literally dance around the kitchen with your spouse. But it's time to get on with other, more mundane chores, so you tack the brochure up on the refrigerator with a happy-face magnet.

Days go by, and even though you've lovingly touched the brochures, you've really been too busy to sit down and really study them. More days go by, then weeks. One day you notice that the brochures have slipped out from underneath their happy-face magnet and are sitting crumpled on the floor. You carefully smooth them out as you think about work, your limited vacation time, the kids' sports schedules, bills, your spouse's new promotion, and, with a sigh, you gently put the brochures in the trash. And instead of some exotic trip, later in the summer you end up spending a week at the shore or in the mountains—maybe.

What this story illustrates is that you had a need—a need to take an exotic trip. Instead, other things got in the way, and the trip got postponed while you tended to other important life matters. What makes you think this doesn't happen to customers, too? Customers may have a need; once you establish it, it's up to you to keep them on track and not let them get distracted by other, everyday matters. That, too, is an element of the question-and-listening techniques a CSR must learn so that an otherwise eager customer doesn't fall by the wayside. The CSR wants the customer to pay attention to his queries and recommendations so that the relationship can grow.

In essence, for management, what the quarter-half-quarter model advocates is shifting the relationship responsibility to the CSR. Of course, different companies have different experiences with moving into this mode, depending on the corporate structure as well as the product or service that's being sold. Bernie Coley, national accounts manager for the U.S. Postal Service, has been slowly reinventing the organization's sales approach for five major national accounts. Let's replay a conversation with Bernie about his experiences, as well as his frustrations:

"What I'm trying to do is get one person to be assigned to an account. We need to personalize the relationship so we know how our business customer operates," he says. I'd like to comment here. His idea certainly makes sense. What better way to meet your customer's needs than to get to know how your customer operates so that you can better understand those needs and, eventually, offer smart solutions? Isn't that what the traditional management consultant does? Bernie wants to transform his traditional CSR into an expert on a specific client's requirements so that the organization can present itself as a "one-stop shop." I've heard that goal stated over and over again. Remember Polaroid's and MCI's case studies about shifting their CSRs into the sales team? Unfortunately, I've also talked to company sales managers who understand the necessity to move into that direction but aren't quite sure how to get there. Bernie's frustration, he told me, is that, "as a service, we should be more integrated."

That's why he wants some kind of road map, what he calls "a consistent program," a formula that his staff can follow to accomplish his goal. And, let's face it, a strategy that is written on paper is much simpler to sell to the top decision-making execs than an unproved idea. Look again at the quarter-half-quarter model, and listen once again to Bernie: "Relationship selling is really what makes the big sales happen. Otherwise you have to stick with the smaller sales."

In Bernie's case, that could mean the difference between a $5,000 to $10,000 sale compared with a potential $10 million to $20 million sale. "Questions help build a relationship. By asking questions, it tells the customer, 'Here's somebody who's interested in my company.'" And it builds trust between the customer and the inside sales person, probably one of the most important aspects of a successful sales relationship. Bernie clearly understands the "probing question" aspect of the quarter-half-quarter model, but, as with most major corporations, it's still going to take his organization some time to get there.

I am frequently skeptical when someone describes a new program or approach and doesn't explain how to execute it or answer the simple question Does it work? So, too, at this point, you may be wondering how to implement the elements of the quarter-half-quarter model and asking, "Does it really work?" I'm going to ask you to take a giant leap of faith here and simply tell you that it does. But I'm not going to assume that you should just take my word for it.

In the following chapters a variety of company executives tell your their stories to illustrate how they've moved their CSRs into active sales roles and why they believe that it's working. And, of course, I'll be peppering the narrative with my recommendations on how the quarter-half-quarter model can aid companies in their quests to build their bottom line through these newly charged CSRs. So stay tuned.

4

"This Is Why I'm Calling"

Crossing Bridges to Create Opportunities

There are probably dozens of clichés about opportunity: It knocks, presents itself, comes through the door, is just around the corner, and so on. But we all know that in real-life sales, we have to create our own opportunities. Oh, sure, sometimes an exciting opportunity does indeed pop up unexpectedly—the guy you met at the gym who's been sweating next to you for months happens to express his frustrations one morning about his search for a new telephone system, setting up the opportunity for you to exchange business cards and put the sales wheels in motion—but it's usually up to us.

For the most part, the seasoned salespeople I know are used to the task of getting down to business and can smell an opportunity to make a sale a mile away. But what about your newly minted inside sales force, the people who are used to asking customers the obvious questions: "Can I help you?" "When do you need delivery?" "Is there anything else I can help you with?" As I discussed earlier, we want our CSRs to ask probing questions actively, to uncover the customer's needs and to learn about the guts of his operations in order to develop a stronger relationship that can eventually lead to increased sales.

For companies still in the process of moving their CSRs into a more active role, this may mean creating the right kind of environment and actually restructuring the sales operations to accommodate and support these new activities before they can really take off. Let's look at how Polaroid, the film and photo equipment maker, approached this situation, and then we'll get into more specifics about the art of asking good questions. Let's revisit Fred Tunney, Polaroid's sales training manager, to hear his story:

"This process dates back about two years ago," Tunney begins. "We established a Customer Care Center and brought many different resources all together under one roof and one management. There's roughly a couple of hundred people there. The whole psychology is to set up the communications center to serve customers that we're no longer able to reach with our salespeople."

Let me interject some explanation here. Fred told me that the company was looking for a way to do more with less. The company had gone through a downsizing, which eliminated about 1,600 jobs, about 20 percent of which involved sales and marketing. At the same time, the company was phasing in TQO—total quality ownership. Because it just made better economic sense, it wanted to focus person-to-person sales efforts on the larger accounts and group its smaller customers under one umbrella through its telephone sales. With this approach, the outside salespeople are freed up to go after the larger customers without the company's sacrificing its long-time smaller customers, like the camera shop in your neighborhood. Altogether, there are between 2,000 and 2,500 smaller customers, which represent a healthy chunk of business, that are now served by its Customer Care Center. Now I'll let Fred continue:

"Our mind-set was to offer better customer care in general. Every customer at every stage needs to be taken care of. So in our Customer Care Center we brought in Polaroid Express (our telesales organization), order services (our order entry and logistics group), customer and technical service, and credit and finance. In addition, we brought in sales, marketing, and personnel training, who were all focused on specific customer needs. So all our orders and all our telesales people now are available to the smaller dealers, and we can make it easier for them to be profitable. It's true one-stop shopping for each customer, so customers can call in orders, ask for the status of their orders, check their credit lines, and get information on the marketing program."

Through still in its infancy, Polaroid's Customer Care Center seems to be achieving its objective. The salespeople are still responsible for the customers served through the Care Center, and the customers like this change in service because Polaroid is stressing the service part of the transition and following through. "We feel that the creation of the CCC has allowed us to focus on the unique needs of different kinds of customers, and we continue to make improvements based on customer feedback and technological advances," Fred tells me.

The next step is for Polaroid to help its customer-service-reps-turned-inside-sales-team learn how to ask good questions so that they can engage customers and uncover their needs. This is the same kind of advanced training that salespeople have been working on for the past few years—a means to differentiate oneself as well as one's product from the competition. And it certainly makes sense to acquaint CSRs with the advanced questioning techniques because, after all, they're one of the few groups of employees who already operate in the customer-solving frame of mind.

Understanding What Your Customer Is Really Saying

In this section, I'll introduce you to the advanced questioning skills that will enable you to generate a greater, more in-depth response from existing, as well as prospective, customers. Obviously, these skills are helpful to anyone involved in sales, so pay attention, because, yes, I will be asking questions later, if not sooner.

Based upon the development of consultative relationships, this strategy is designed to teach you and your CSRs how to create and ask four different types of questions to focus on the customer's real needs—a benchmark for the entire approach.

Determine Intent

The first step is to create a selling opportunity by truly understanding what the customer is saying to you. Customers may say all kinds of different things about the reason for their phone call and respond with some pat answers when you think you're really selling your product to them. I call these "buying signals"—comments customers make that lead you to think they're ready to sign on.

Here comes that first test for CSRs as well as salespeople. I want you to list as many customer comments as you can, "buying signals" that customers have said to you in the past that you believed expressed their interest in your products or service. Don't worry about giving wrong answers. Just list what you can easily recall, or what you've heard over and over again.

To start you off, consider "Sounds good; let's talk about your idea next week." Now, it's your turn:

MOST COMMON CUSTOMER COMMENTS

1. _____

2. _____

3. _____

4. _____

5. _____

6. _____

7. _____

8. _____

9. _____

10. _____

I am tempted to say, "Put down your pencils," but I'm not timing this. Now review your comments. The customer may have talked about the weather or his son's sledding accident before he eventually got to the point of his phone call. He's got a problem, and, as usual, he's looking to you for answers, solutions, or some kind of help, whether he's asking if you have number four gaskets in stock or wants you to give him his current billing status. The point is that you have to train yourself to listen carefully to what the customer is saying because that serves as the foundation for moving from the reactive mode into the active one and creating a bona fide selling opportunity, what I have dubbed "bridging" for CSRs. Bridging is a mind-set that governs how you look at a situation and then act on it.

For example, let's consider again the customer requesting number four gaskets. It won't take long for you to realize that he has a problem and needs your help. You may ask him how his company is using them, how long they usually last (you probably know what they're spending if you pull up the customer's records), and whether he's aware that your company now makes a comparable, more technologically advanced version of that gasket-using machine. How many of the older models do they have in operation? I think you get the idea. You listened to his request and saw an opportunity to move from simply filling his order for number four gaskets to gathering information on how his organization uses the replacement product, taking the opportunity to pitch your company's newer model.

He says to you, "That sounds great. I like what you're telling me. I never knew you had those machines." Gosh, this guy has really indicated interest. Good for you. You've sold him the new machines. But have you?

A traditional CSR response would have been to check the company's inventories on number four gaskets, ask the customer how many he wants, and fill the order. You might have completed the conversation by asking if he needs anything else. After a brief pause, he would say no, you'd thank him, and that would have been the end until he needed more gaskets, maybe several months from now.

What's wrong with this picture? Right—the CSR may have

listened to the customer's request, but there was no analysis there to try to best meet the customer's demands. The CSR didn't successfully cross the bridge. Neither did the customer, for that matter. It sounds to me as if the customer needs a more reliable machine that doesn't depend upon a gasket. (I confess. The only machine I'm aware of that uses a gasket is a refrigerator, and I doubt that's what the customer's industrial equipment really needed, but it served to make my point. If there is some industrial machine out there that uses a number four gasket, please let me know.)

Back to the point. The reason for this little exercise was to help you to realize that to create new opportunities, it's important to listen to and really understand your customer's needs. Probably more important, in your new role you really need to also understand what the customer's comments really mean so that you don't go off half-cocked when the customer hasn't really made a sales commitment to you, as far as he's concerned.

Now, let's return to your list of the most common customer comments. I bet you have some variation on the example I gave: "That sounds good. I like what you're talking about. I never knew you had those systems." This question is for the veteran sellers. How many times have you heard a similar comment but still didn't make the sale? Probably more times than you'd like to remember, right? But for CSRs, in your new role, you need to understand what your customer is legitimately saying. That's why it's important to separate these comments into three distinct categories—negative, noncommittal, and positive (see Figure 4-1). Even though your customer has indicated some interest in your product or service, is she really interested in buying? Does she say the same things to your competition? Are you just guessing at what she means? These three categories can help you gauge your customer's interest. Let me give you my definitions first. A negative comment indicates disinterest, skepticism, and/or resistance. A noncommittal remark indicates an impartial attitude toward your idea/solution. A positive comment displays a supportive, encouraging, or optimistic position where an intent of action is present.

OK. Got that? Here's another exercise for you.

Figure 4-1.   Three categories of customer comments.

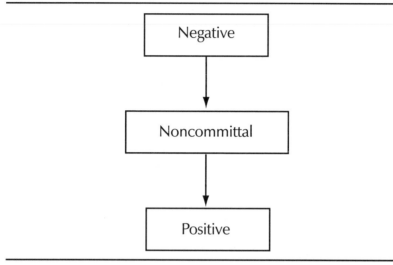

CATEGORIZING EXERCISE

Assess the following as either: N = Negative; NC = Noncommittal;
P = Positive
      Circle the correct response.

1.	What is your product availability?	N	NC	P
2.	I like the idea. I'll talk to my manager about it.	N	NC	P
3.	*[If in person] Customer leans towards you.*	N	NC	P
4.	Sounds good. What's your discount for multiple orders?	N	NC	P
5.	This will help achieve our goals of increasing revenue.	N	NC	P
6.	I like it, but I need to get approval because we've merged recently with another company.	N	NC	P
7.	Your proposal looks good. I need time to compare it to the others. Call me next week.	N	NC	P

8.	Your people really seem to understand our situation.	N	NC	P
9.	You tell a convincing story.	N	NC	P
10.	I'm interested in hearing more, but I'm leaving town today. Please call me next week.	N	NC	P

Now let's analyze these comments. I'd say they all sound pretty good, pretty convincing. They could be all positive. But they're not.

In *number 1* the customer sounds as if he's already signed on the bottom line. However, this is a noncommittal question because there is no intent to actually move ahead to the next phase.

Number 2 also sounds positive, but does it really indicate a solid intention to buy? Nope. Besides, we don't really know who his manager is. Does he have the authority to make decisions?

Number 3, "customer leans toward you," is obviously for face-to-face encounters, which could happen for a CSR depending upon how a company structures its inside sales operation. Remember that MCI paired up its CSRs with its outside sales team, and they made some sales calls together. You might find yourself in a similar situation.

If you've ever read any of those body language books that have been around for a while (I recall a series of research studies performed several years ago by the body language guru Edward Hall), you know that certain gestures have certain meanings. For example, if a person crosses his arms, in body language that's interpreted as a closing-out gesture. The arm-crosser is shutting you out. However, that may also simply be a comfortable position for him, or maybe he's got a sore arm from a particularly rough game of handball that morning. There's no intention to action here, either. So a customer who leans toward you is non-committal, not positive.

Number 4, "Sounds good. What's your discount for multiple orders?," really sounds positive. He's already adding up the numbers in his head and figuring how the result might fit in with his budget, right? Wrong. Again, he hasn't indicated any intention of buying from you. In fact, he may be checking your deal with a proposal he received from your competition. Or, maybe he's just curious how you discount your products to get some ideas on how he might discount his. So this is a noncommittal response.

Number 5, "This will help achieve our goals of increasing revenue," may be an honest response, but it's hardly a commitment—so would buying a new division, or selling one off, or simply selling more stuff. It's certainly not a positive statement because there's no intention to do business with you.

Number 6 is a bit more transparent, and I would hope that only the most naive CSR would fall for it. Otherwise, it's obviously a noncommittal statement for the same reasons stated earlier—there's no indication of intent to act.

By now, I'm assuming you're picking up a trend with these comments. Yes, they are all noncommittal statements, even though most of them sound positive on the surface. The lesson to be learned here is simple—listen carefully for a sign of intent of action. If it's not there, the comment isn't positive, even though the specific words the customer uses, which we've always associated with positive situations, may convey signs of positive intent. Words such as "good," "like," "understand" can be positive out of context—"good dog," "I like you," "I understand you." But in a selling situation, you have to look at the entire statement before making any judgment calls. Bear in mind, too, that your customer might be making the same comments to your competition just to keep everyone off base and to get the best price. That's why I can't stress strongly enough the importance of looking for "intent of action."

Like these example statements, most customer statements are noncommittal. Certainly, it's a lot easier to detect negative comments, like the ones I use with that telemarketing person who keeps calling my house at dinnertime to offer me a new credit card—"I'm not interested."

Watch Out for "Masking"

After determining intent, your next step for truly understanding what your customer is saying is being aware of what I call "masking." I define masking as not revealing one's actual feelings. This element always reminds me of what happened when my wife and I were first dating. I've always been an Indy car fanatic. In fact, I don't tell too many people this, but I fantasize that in my next life I'll come back as Al Unser, Jr., one of my racing car idols. Friends always ask me how I can possibly enjoy watching a car go around and around a track. Well, I can. I love the speed and the technology. Now, my wife (then my girlfriend) was well aware of my infatuation with racing cars, but you know that old Ann Landers line, "she thought he would change." Anyway, one day I came flying over to her house excitedly telling her about a big Indy car race that I had just heard about. I remember her response as if it were said yesterday: "That sounds great. I'm really interested. Why don't you get all the details?" You can imagine how excited I was. So I ran out and bought two penthouse tickets for $300.

Well, I guess you know what happened. As it turns out, she doesn't enjoy Indy car racing. After several years of marriage, I've learned that if I ask her to go somewhere and she says, "Sounds great. I'm really interested, so why don't you get all the details?" I know there's no way that she wants to go. And that is probably the best illustration I can give you of masking. People just hate to say no. It's so final. Besides, it might hurt someone's feelings or upset him. Later, when I asked my wife why she didn't tell me she didn't want to go to the race, she told me she didn't want to douse my enthusiasm. And, besides, she thought that maybe the idea would grow on her. So she purposely left the door open.

Think about some of your own experiences. Recently a friend's daughter wanted desperately to go to the high school semiformal and found "the perfect dress." So mom went to the store with her to look at it. Seeing it on the rack, my friend already had her doubts, but once her daughter tried it on, my friend almost died. It had practically no back and looked as if it were painted on her. She could only guess at her husband's reaction. Granted, the girl looked terrific in it, and by the glowing smile on her face my friend could tell she really wanted this dress. How could she say no? Well, looking at the price tag helped, but her daughter rarely asks for something even close to this expensive. However, my friend had no intention of letting her teenage daughter walk out of the house with that dress on. Instead, she said, "Yes, sweetheart. It does look terrific on you.

For that matter, almost any dress would look terrific on you. In fact, the other day I saw some beautiful gowns in the window of a store down the street. Let's look at them, too, before making a final decision."

My friend, in a moment of desperation, masked her true feelings because she didn't want to say no to her daughter. Now, let's transfer the elements of these two stories to what our CSR is learning about building his relationship with his customer and understanding what the customer is really saying. If we combine masking with positive responses as we discussed earlier, is it possible that your customer could be making the same remarks to someone else, such as your competition? Certainly. And could he really be saying just the opposite of what you think you heard? Yep. Now, think back to the noncommittal statements. Are noncommittal statements more common than you realized, and could customers be responding with more noncommittal statements than any other kind? Absolutely.

A Model for Pacing the Sales Conversation

As these illustrations have shown, our society has sensitized us to making noncommittal statements and taught us to accept them as positive, because they're clearly not negative. Since we were children, our parents have admonished us to be nice to other people and not to hurt their feelings. But that age-old approach to understanding what someone is telling us just won't cut it anymore with customers. It's our way of saying, "I like you." Haven't you ever been in a clothing store and kept a sales clerk busy while you tried on several dresses or suits? Then, you glanced at your watch and saw that you needed to get back to your office, so you said to the poor clerk, "Can you hold this one? I'll be back for it," knowing darn well that you wouldn't be. Or perhaps a telemarketer has called you during the dinner hour and once she began her spiel, you said, "I'm in the middle of dinner. Can you call me back another time?"

What's the point of this? Simple. Because we tend to interpret these pat, noncommittal statements, which carry no intention of action, as positive statements and because of the masking phenomenon, we jump right in and begin explaining our product or service. But, and most important, your customer hasn't yet seen the need to change well-established buying habits and purchase your product. And the customer may view you as too pushy or too aggressive. That's why it's critical that CSRs learn to distinguish the difference between noncommittal and positive responses and become well versed in how to build a relationship on these elements.

What this listening lesson has been leading up to is the basic guiding principle of this entire approach, which I discussed in Chapter 3. I call it the quarter-half-quarter model because it guides you in pacing your sales conversation (see Figure 4-2). Modeled after a clock face, it shows you when to apply the steps of consultative selling and provides a sequence and an emphasis for each part of the selling process. In other words, it's a technique that effectively holds your hand while you're selling your customer.

The model calls for half of the time spent with a customer to be used for "building relationships" tactics—understanding

Figure 4-2. Pacing your sales conversation.

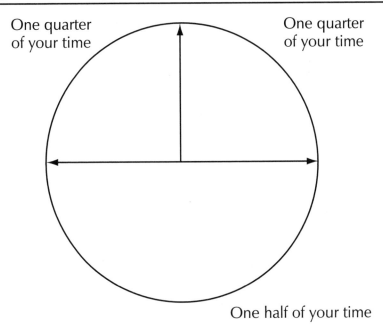

One quarter of your time

One quarter of your time

One half of your time

the customer's real needs, uncovering new opportunities, and creating a need for change; the remaining time is distributed equally between opening the sales call and presenting your solutions and closing.

Before we launch into a more thorough study of the quarter-half-quarter model, it's imperative that you understand that no system or approach (remember your college exams) will work unless you prepare for it in an orderly fashion. Don't try to cram, because the key to your success is tied to how well you are prepared; research prior to the call is essential for creating the proper atmosphere, relationship, and credibility. Gather your background information from your company's database resources, such as the Internet.

Bridging

In a famous poem by Robert Frost, "The Road Not Taken," the poet comes to a fork in the road and has to decide which way he's going to go. His horse is trying to lead the way, but he's not sure he should listen to it. No, I'm not going literary on you. But the poem contains elements that relate to this process. It's a cold, snowy night, and if the protagonist makes the wrong choice, he could run into serious trouble. Fortunately, CSRs have a road map to help them find the way. They just have to read it correctly and follow "the road not taken." For CSRs, this needs to be the automatic approach, because, more often than not, CSRs have been used to building relationships by responding to customers and solving their problems. So they need to choose the less-traveled CSR road and head toward establishing opportunities. I call this "bridging." CSRs are used to operating on one side of the bridge—responding to customer phone calls—but now they must move to the other side of the bridge, making phone calls and selling (Figure 4-3).

Think of bridging as a transition. A psychologist I know uses the term to describe the teenage years—they're a bridge between childhood and adulthood. In our case, it's a means of moving your mind-set, as well as that of the customer, into a selling situation. I know that, as a CSR, you probably handle hundreds of phone calls a day from customers asking for infor-

Figure 4-3. Bridging.

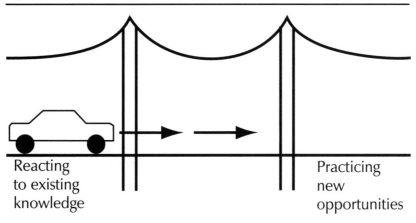

Reacting to existing knowledge

Practicing new opportunities

mation or needing something from you. Remember that they need something from you. But that kind of need is not what an inside sales team really wants ultimately to fulfill. That's why bridging presents two challenges for the salesperson, and for the customer, whether he knows it or not.

The bridging challenge for CSRs is to readjust their mind-sets and adopt a new, active approach. The bridging challenge for customers is to move into different mind-sets when they deal with the CSRs. Of course, phone rapport—focusing on the elements of the quarter-half-quarter model—will help direct that change. This may should a bit cumbersome to you, but I assure you that you're not alone in this transition process. Due to corporate changes over the past few years—mergers, downsizing, new product acquisitions, management techniques—literally thousand of employees have found themselves walking the same path or, as I've called it, bridge. Think about a pharmaceutical salesperson who has been used to selling one class of drugs, such as cardiac medications; now he also has to sell antidepressants. What a state he's in! He has to add a whole new targeted customer group, while also learning about the product line and why it's superior, and so on. But I know many salespeople who have had to make this transition, and they've succeeded.

Customers have always thought of CSRs in a singular role, representing a certain kind of service. Let's say a CSR works for a telecommunications company and Joe-the-Customer for many years has been purchasing his long-distance telephone services from that company. But now it's also offering local phone services, which it is trying to cross-sell him. Now, he knows the company as a long-distance supplier; it has credibility with him, and that's his image of the company. In addition, he's had a relationship with another local phone calling company for years. Naturally, he's skeptical of the new service because it doesn't have a local-service track record with him. What should the CSR do?

Let's look at another situation. Maybe you work at the U.S. Postal Service, and every day a customer uses the regular mailing service. But more recently the post office has been promoting its version of overnight delivery service, a niche that has been almost locked up by companies like Federal Express and UPS. I know that when I hand my secretary a package and tell her to put it in the mail, she automatically sends it by FedEx; when I ask her why, she says that's what the customer wants. As in the previous example, the customer is happy with his current vendor and is comfortable with its track record.

These stories illustrate habits, and we all know that it's difficult to alter habits, especially ones we've engaged in for years—overeating, smoking, drinking coffee, and on and on. But that's what the CSR is asking a customer to do when she tries to cross-sell him her company's newest product or service—change his buying habits. I know when I send out my hundreds of direct-mail pieces every year to promote my seminar series, I automatically tell my secretary—"Send them U.S. Postal Service."

I don't want you to get the impression that convincing your customers to change how they view your company is some kind of Herculean task, because you do have a major advantage over your competition. Your customers know you. You've got a continuing access to them. They take your phone calls. And why? Because you've always been viewed as a solution to their problems (I consider it a problem when you need a new order of a product in order to keep your machines humming and your employees working). So how do you take advantage of this situation? Like real estate investors, you leverage it. Use it. Exploit it. That's how you'll succeed in your own bridging and that of your clients.

I confess. I'm not claiming that changing your modus operandi is simple. That bridge is no flat, smooth surface. Roller blades aren't allowed, either, and it's important to pay careful attention to where you're stepping while displaying confidence in yourself. Again, my psychologist friend recommends an excellent method to help you adopt change that may be intimidating. Try picturing yourself in a situation where you've been uncomfortable, yet found a method to make yourself comfortable. I'm sure you've all attended some kind of fancy event—a banquet, fund-raiser, friend-of-your-mother's wedding—where you were seated with strangers. How do you start a conversation? What do you say to complete strangers? You might ramble on or tend to say whatever pops into your head first—the weather, the room's decor, the food—what my friend's teenage daughter tends to call "dumb stuff." Then you notice a table of friends happily chatting away. You run over to talk to them. This situation is certainly comfortable. But what if your friends weren't there? Then you cross back over the bridge and talk to the strangers. You'd probably end up getting details about their lives—what they do for a living, where they live, their hobbies— and you might even discover that you like them.

By now you've probably figured out why I've been telling you these little vignettes. There are certainly more opportunities out there in what I'll call the "uncomfortable zone" than in your standard comfort zone. You can probably think of dozens.

Let's replay this last situation with a road map for how to start a conversation with strangers. You certainly don't need to ask about the weather, because your road map (in this case, a conversation guide) will lead you along the way.

The Opener

Let's more closely examine the composition of the first quarter— "the opener." This step focuses the call and makes the proper impression on the customer. It contains as many as five parts to provide direction, build rapport, gain control, and generate interest in what you can do. But sometimes the customer, perhaps unwittingly, throws roadblocks in your path through his noncommittal statements. For example, (and this will surely apply to seasoned salespeople), have you ever introduced an idea, only to have the customer say, "I'm really busy. Make it quick. What specials do you have today?" or "I'm really satisfied with my current vendor," or "I heard some great things about your company. Tell me all about it." You know what the customer is doing to you? He's pushing you to offer him a solution—now—and pulling you from the first quarter of the quarter-half-quarter model into the last quarter (Figure 4-4). If you do start to present your solution too early in the process, who's really talking, you or the customer? Even though you may be saying more, the customer is effectively talking—he's in charge of the process.

Remember that UCLA study mentioned in Chapter 3, that said your words affect people only 7 percent of the time? The odds are that 93 percent of your words aren't making an impact on the customer at all. But let's say that while you're giving your "little talk," you end up giving him your solution, yet you're still

Figure 4-4.   Jumping from the first quarter to the last.

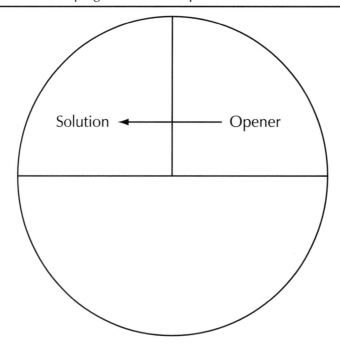

trying to get a commitment from him. He says, "Sounds good. Send me the information." You then make the mistake of viewing his remarks as positive and encouraging. But, if you haven't secured a commitment from him, you may as well be stuck in quicksand—the more you move, the more you get stuck.

The most important aspect that the customer is able to get during this opening phase should be a relationship, not the product, but, unfortunately, you may jump past that part by not trying to create the relationship. If you don't ask the right questions, you won't control the conversation. The customer will. You're not selling the right agenda, and you're ignoring the purpose of the model—to pace the sale and control it. Of course, all is not completely lost. If the customer does succeed in pushing you to the last quarter, you can always move to the half section of the model. The model is flexible, so there's no reason you have to stay in the final quarter if you don't want to be there (Figure 4-5).

Figure 4-5.　A flexible system.

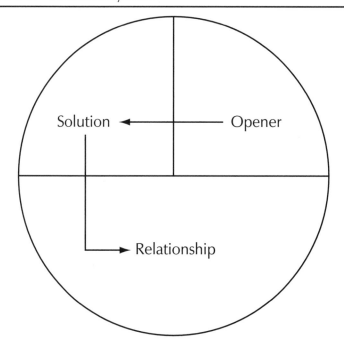

To execute the opening part of the quarter-half-quarter model, I suggest using as many of the five components of the opener (Figure 4-6) as you need. I've illustrated the most complicated ones for you. The components are:

Introduction	Identification of yourself, your company, and the product/service being sold
Common Ground	Statement or question surrounding business and/or personal events affecting the customer
Reason/Agenda	Statement of the topics to be discussed during your conversation

Figure 4-6.   Five components of the opener.

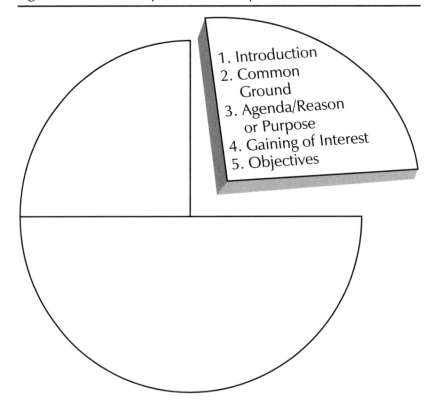

1. Introduction
2. Common Ground
3. Agenda/Reason or Purpose
4. Gaining of Interest
5. Objectives

Gaining Interest	A hook, indicating a benefit to the customer, for encouraging feedback and time commitment
Objective	A measurable goal projecting your intentions upon the completion of the call/conversation (i.e., identifying the next step)

Using these steps as guides, you can build rapport with customers, tell them what you hope to accomplish, and put yourself on the right track. The components will give you a key element necessary for establishing a partnering relationship buy-in from customers.

Introduction and Common Ground

You probably won't need to start from scratch with the first component if you've just received a service call from the customer; I assume you've already exchanged pleasantries because you know each other. You're probably at the point of establishing common ground between yourself and the customer. Even if the customer is calling you, you can still jump into the first-quarter mode and make a request from her for assistance while assuring her that this won't take long. Try "I really hope you can help me. I'll be brief." Probably nine out of ten times the customer will say something like, "Sure, but make it quick." Then you can go into the reason for your call, saying, "I wanted to talk to you because. . . ."

Why did I emphasize the word "because"? Because (oops!) it's more than just a grammatical link. Have you ever read the book *Influence and Persuasion—How and Why People Do Things*? It's by an Arizona State University professor, and I read it in graduate school. It's fascinating. He explains a series of research studies he conducted on how to influence people. One I particularly like is a study of 100 test trials conducted at the school library. A male freshman, a regular-looking guy, was standing in line at a copying machine. There were ten people in line ahead of him. He moved to the front of the line, saying, "Excuse me. I have to make a copy." He was successful about 30 percent of the time in moving to the front of the line. The next time he tried moving to the front of the line, he said, "Excuse me. I have to make a copy because I'm late for my class." Out of 100 trials, he was successful in moving to the front of the line 80 percent of the time. Perhaps he was that successful because the other students could all relate to being late for a class.

In another trial, the student just said, "Excuse me. I really have to make a copy because I have to make a copy." This time he was successful 70 percent of the time. The professor concluded that when the student used the word "because" and gave a reason for his need to jump to the head of the line, he influenced people. The lesson to be learned here is that when you call a client or he calls you and you use "because" to make your point, you're more likely to get a positive response—for example, "I was reading an article in *Newsweek* magazine recently about the drought in California, and because much of your raw materials come from there, I was wondering how this was affecting your business." Or, "I just heard about a survey of purchasing managers who were predicting an upturn in the economy because purchase orders rose 8 percent in the last quarter. Has your company experienced that kind of increase, too?"

I really gave you a bit of a freebie with these two questions because they also contain what I call multilayered probing questions (MLPQs), a technique that governs the half of the quarter-half-quarter model. I'll go into more detail on MLPQs later, but you can see how they work together with "because." For this exercise, that simple word carries a lot of weight with it. It grabs a person's attention, and he wants to hear what's coming next. Of course, my toddler's response to "Why won't you eat your green beens?" is also "because," but that's another story entirely.

Before we leave the first-quarter opener, let me introduce a variation on that theme, called the Reactive Opener. In this case, there's no introduction necessary, but before the customer hangs up, jump in and say, "Do you mind if I ask you another quick question? I was reading an article the other day [you can use one of the situation examples given earlier] and I wondered how does this compare with what you're experiencing?" No matter how the customer responds, you can follow with "tell me more" if he says his company isn't experiencing that problem, or you can say, "The article suggested others are concerned with this dilemma. What are your thoughts on this?"

Reason or Purpose/Agenda

Once the customer is done responding to your question, you can move on to the third component of the opener. It's up to the CSR to quickly state her agenda to the customer. Consider this sample agenda: Agenda Comments/Questions.

First, talk about what's happening in the industry, as we did, using an article, survey, or other report as your foundation. Then say, "I'd like to talk to you about that." Ask quick questions to see what the customer has experienced, adding, "Let me share with you what we've been doing to help many companies with the same problems. This shouldn't take more than a few minutes. After I ask you a couple of questions, I'd like to tell you what we have to offer you, and you might want to know about it." I didn't time this, but if it took more than thirty seconds I'd be surprised. Obviously, CSRs need not use these exact words but can simply follow the theme for setting an agenda, and letting customers know that they won't be taking up much of their time. This approach works in any situation—selling a product or service or responding to a problem call.

Your agenda, however, does not include selling the product. You're not there yet. You're building interest by selling issues. Earlier you asked the customer questions about the California drought. That's an issue. You're still asking questions to gather information on what's important to the customer, setting your stage for the close. Remember the customer needs to know what a product does, not what it is. So what if it is the first pink widget on the market? What's important is that it prevents anyone from breaking into your car.

Objectives

Now that you've gone through the introduction, established some common ground and set an agenda, you're ready to "set the anchor," as I like to call it, because this description connotes stability. When a ship is anchored, it sways back and forth only with the tide. If anchored properly, it won't float away from the dock. For the past few pages we've been discussing different ways of maintaining stability and control so that the customer can't drag you into the last quarter before you've completed the elements of the first quarter. One final point on that note—your customer's excitement or eagerness. Although the customer may sound raring to move ahead, have you received any kind of agreement, any indication of intent for action? If not, don't let the customer's enthusiasm drag you into the last quarter. Remember, you cannot omit the agenda and objectives, and not until the customer has agreed to these factors have you truly completed the first quarter so that you can move on to the half.

In Chapter 5, I discuss how you can enlist your customer in a productive conversation by using the various questioning techniques described in the "half" portion of the quarter-half-quarter model—informational, dialogue-probing, countering, and multilayered (MLPQ). If you haven't already detected it, I'm stating right here that asking the right kinds of questions can make or break your selling approach. By definition, you ask questions to gather information—"Where are you going?," "When will you be home?," "What's for dinner?," "What time is that meeting?" You probably ask thousands of questions of your family, friends, customers, and coworkers every day. Those are questions. Those I discuss in Chapter 5 are QUESTIONS. So let's move ahead and discuss how you can become an expert at questioning your customers to meet your selling goals—the heart of the "half" part of the quarter-half-quarter model.

5

"Please Share With Me How Quickly You Pay Your Invoices Compared With a Year Ago"

Using Dialogue-Probing and Related Questioning Techniques

Remember back in high school, or perhaps college, when you had to memorize a Shakespearean dialogue? It might have been from *Romeo and Juliet*, *A Midsummer Night's Dream*, *Julius Caesar*, or *Hamlet*. Because it was pounded over and over into your head, I bet you still remember parts of it ("Et tu, Brute?"). For the life of me I'll never understand why we had to go through that exercise. I have yet to run into a sales situation that required a Shakespeare recitation, but I do recall that my prospective customers sure asked a lot of questions. In fact, sometimes those questions went on for pages. I'm not exactly proposing that you recite your questions in a Shakespearean tone, although that could be interesting. I can just hear you asking a customer whom you are having trouble reaching, "Mario, Mario, wherefore art thou, Mario?" That certainly would be an attention-getter. But I am suggesting you choose and use questioning techniques that will not only gather information, like those used by Shakespeare's characters, but also help lead the customer to making a sales commitment.

That's why I designed the quarter-half-quarter model to contain mostly questioning techniques, which account for the largest segment (from 3:00 to 9:00 on the clock face) and are expected to account for half of the sales call (Figure 5-1). These series of questions are designed to help you understand the customer's real needs and uncover new opportunities. To do this, we need to examine the kinds of questions salespeople ask on a regular basis, which I call open and closed informational, dialogue-probing, countering, and multilayered probing questions

Figure 5-1.   Questioning techniques as part of the quarter-half-quarter model.

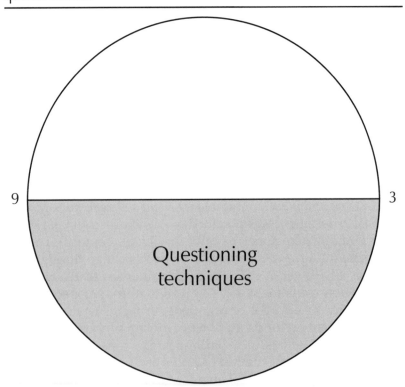

(MLPQs). I know this is not the first time someone has pointed to the importance of proper structuring of your customer-questioning techniques. You've probably heard a colleague, manager, or mentor talk about the need to ask the right questions so that you can engage your customer in a productive conversation. This conversation not only reveals basic information but also uncovers confidential, hard-to-get information that will separate your customer relationship and solutions from the rest of your competitors.

Recital vs. Dialogue Questions

OK, it's pencil time again. I'd like you to identify the ten most common questions you ask your customers. I'll even give you space to write them down, because we'll be returning to them later to evaluate them in different contexts.

QUESTIONS   R/D

1. _____

2. _____

3. _____

4. _____

5. _____

6. _____

7. _____

8. _____

9. _____

10. _____

Like many of you, I used to think that a question was a question was a question. Of course, I've since learned differently. Back when I was in graduate school studying training and development, my professor (who loved to stick me with the most agonizing projects) asked me to dig through twenty years' worth of research for him. Did I want to do this? Of course not. Did I cheerfully say yes? Of course I did. I was a lowly grad student who needed to stay on the professor's good side. As it turned out, the data I had to review concerned the concept of open and closed questions. These kinds of questions elicit only yes or no answers or offer only a simple choice. Most everyday conversations are composed of open and closed questions.

Well, as I continued digging through the research, mumbling to myself how I wasn't learning a single useful thing, I stumbled across an article by the educator Meredith Gall that compared dialogue and recall-oriented recitation questions. Now this piqued my curiosity. The article suggested that open and closed questions were ineffective and obsolete, yet almost every major sales training program was based on them. How could open and closed questions be obsolete? If they were, what else could you do? The article said that open and closed questions get the conversation going but that, in order to gather details, you have to engage the customer in an in-depth dialogue. It recommended that salespeople not get all bent out of shape over asking open and closed questions but instead focus on whether a question calls for recital or is a dialogue-probing question. The article encouraged salespeople to try something new without making themselves, or CSRs, feel like that TV character Herb from the old TV sitcom *WKRP in Cincinnati*, who dressed in obnoxious, mismatched plaid suits and couldn't sell a cookie to Cookie Monster even if he tried.

Recital and dialogue questions do differ dramatically from the usual open and closed questions. Come to think of it, maybe Herb wouldn't get it after all, because this does require you to think. A recital question is defined as a recurring sequence of seller questions in response to which the customer recites what he already knows. The most revealing part of the definition of dialogue questions is that they create comparisons that stimulate new thinking and lead to change. The questions solicit opinions and thoughts, not just correct answers (Figure 5-2).

Before we review the question-asking experiences of some corporate executives, let's go back and review the questions you wrote down earlier. (Thought I'd forgotten, didn't you?) Are your questions recital or dialogue? If you follow the pattern established by the salespeople who attend my seminars and have completed this exercise in the past, I'd guess that more than 80 percent of your questions are recital and the remaining 20 percent are dialogue. What's wrong with that, you ask? Look back at the definitions of recital and dialogue. Recital questions draw out answers that the customer already knows: "How many factories do you operate? How many employees work in that division?" Not only does the customer already know the answers to those questions; you would, too, if you'd taken the trouble to pick up the company's annual report. Besides, the customer may even find you to be boring because your line of questioning, quite frankly, is pretty unexciting. You can lose your edge on the sales call if you ask all the same questions. Where's the variety? On the other hand, remember that dialogue questions offer just that. They stir up the conversation because they ask for opinions and ideas, not just correct answers. After all, you're not giving your customer a test.

To help you easily recall the definitions of each kind of question, think of the recital questions in terms of a dance recital—it's one person performing, a singular situation. For dialogue questions, remember that two people having a conversation is also a dialogue. Dialogues are longer and contain more

Figure 5-2. Two questioning techniques.

Recital

vs.

Dialogue

information. So recital is more of a singular component, and dialogues require two people engaged in a more extensive conversation.

To borrow from one of my favorite old TV dramas (not the
1995 movie), your mission, should you choose to accept it, is to
change those 80/20 recital-versus-dialogue percentages I mentioned earlier. Even a 50/50 accounting of your recital-versus-
dialogue questions is acceptable. My recommendation is to ask
one or two really great dialogue questions in every conversation
in order to draw out your customer and to stimulate his thinking
toward your agenda. Let's see how this can work.

The Four Effective Types of Questions for Consultative Selling

Which professions come to mind when you think about a group
of people who make their living and, for the most part, do a
good job of asking the right questions? No, I'm not talking about
the kids behind the register at the local fast-food joint. What
about lawyers, counselors, and journalists? All of these professionals have the same thing in common—they all understand
the importance of seeking and gaining access to information that
their competition probably doesn't know about, even though
each professional may have a different agenda. For example, a
lawyer's intent might be completely different from, say, a marriage counselor's. And think about journalists. If you have the
good fortune (or misfortune, depending on your situation) to be
interviewed by a reporter or have the opportunity to watch one
in action, good or bad, you can learn a lot about how to ask
effective questions.

One media personality probably all of us have heard or
watched at some time is Barbara Walters. I admit that I happen
to be a fan of hers. I'm always amazed at how she gets people to
say some of the most outlandish things on national TV. In fact, if
you've ever watched one of her interviews, you may have noticed how the people she is interviewing react to her questions.
Some people have even started to cry. Now, that doesn't mean I
recommend you learn how to reduce your customers to tears
because they've done it to you often enough. The point here is

that in almost every one of her interviews, the subject leans back and says something like, "Barbara, I have never said this before." Eureka!

So what do experienced reporters know about the questioning process that CSRs and many salespeople don't know? I have an old friend who's been a newspaper reporter for years. He agrees with my description of questioning: "The key to your success is asking the right questions and listening effectively." Without that, he tells me, you may as well hang it up. For CSRs, effective questions:

- Initiate the consultative process.
- Help build a relationship and an understanding of the customer's position, situation, and needs.

To establish and develop strong consultative relationships, classic questioning and listening skills are no longer sufficient to differentiate you from your competitors. You'll learn how to ask better questions and what to say and listen for when you receive answers from your newly formed questions.

To start this communication process, let's look at each of these major questioning techniques and how they're applied to consultative selling.

Types of Questions Used in Consultative Relationships
1. Open/closed informational
2. Dialogue-probing
3. Countering
4. Multilayered

Try taking a shot at defining open and closed informational questions. Then determine what a misuse of such a question would be, and give an advantage of this kind of question.

OPEN/CLOSED INFORMATIONAL QUESTIONS

Definition _____

Misuse: _____

Advantage: _____

So how'd you do? This may be a bit tough at this point, but some of the answers have already appeared in previous explanations, even though they may not have been specifically labeled as such. Open and closed informational questions are those that seek facts, figures, and detail. They act like recital questions. The misuse is asking too many at one time so that you effectively never uncover new information or opportunities that you don't already know of. The advantage is that they can "warm up" the conversation and make the customer feel comfortable, since he's discussing information that he knows well.

Like anything else, open and closed informational questions have other drawbacks if used improperly. They can be self-serving (you show-off, you); they don't stimulate the customer to see a need for change (we'll get to more on that later); and they don't tell the customer anything about you or your product. In addition, those familiar open and closed questions, if used during an open and closed informational dialogue-probing situation, aren't giving you information that your competition doesn't have. And remember that the whole purpose behind this process is to build a better relationship so that you can outquestion and outsell your competition.

These questioning techniques—open/closed informational, dialogue-probing, countering, and multilayered—are sometimes used consistently and sometimes used only when called for. Let's take a look at another situation (in case you aren't a Barbara Walters fan) that illustrates how one company adopted the consultative questioning techniques and succeeded.

The Impact of Effective Questions—A Case Study

As discussed earlier, accounting is one of the industries that has been forced to shift gears from sitting back and watching clients walk in the door to actively seeking new business. This has required an attitudinal change as well as policy shifts. And the technique? Better questioning. Listen to Lars Mawn, health care services partner with the national accounting firm of Deloitte & Touche, tell his story:

"About fifteen years ago, our business was more about servicing clients, and the focus was not on selling. Today, we are still focused on servicing our clients and exceeding their expectations, but to grow our business we must sell our services. The health care industry is consolidating, so now clients want more service for less money. That has forced us to constantly reengineer the way we service our clients, and the way we sell them."

Let me interject a point here. It's funny. Before I spoke with Lars, I never really gave much thought to how important solid questioning techniques could be to the accounting industry. After all, wouldn't their questions be limited to the audit, such as "Where's the documentation for this expense?" That used to be the case, but obviously it's not anymore. Like many other industries, accounting has been forced to analyze its various products and institute changes in how they approach the growing part of their business—the consulting opportunities. That's what the auditing tasks represent now—an opportunity to learn more about a client's business in order to build upon the consulting assignments. Now, back to Lars.

"The business challenge is going out and obtaining new business while expanding our service with the existing clients. We have to be proactive in continuously learning about the client's business and issues. Typically, the client board of directors engages the accountants, so when we meet the board members we must get a good handle on their expectations. We've learned that probing for information is more effective than asking questions that can be answered with a simple yes or no. To make the most of our questioning technique, we ask questions that are a bit different each time so that we can gather new information. Then when we walk away from that meeting, we're thinking, 'Gee, I hadn't thought about it that way before.' "

It's me again. Do you catch the comparison with CSRs? How about the kinds of questions they ask? In Lars' case, the firm enjoys built-in opportunities for building its business. As we discussed in Chapter 4, CSRs are also offered built-in opportunities. This is another way of looking at it. Like an accounting firm, CSRs are presented with numerous occurrences to talk with the clients under favorable conditions—and not the standard selling environment. It's a different kind of atmosphere for the client.

Not many industries enjoy these built-in sales openings as Deloitte & Touche has discovered. See how this operates, CSRs? Pairing the right kinds of questions with the ease of connecting with the client is an advantage few others enjoy. Think about it. Now I'll let Lars continue.

"Last year, we sat down with the chief financial officer at one of our clients with the intention of updating our understanding of the business issues facing the organization. We asked him, 'From looking at your position a year ago, what was your largest challenge then, and how can you compare it with your current challenges?' We then followed up with, 'What areas was the CEO focusing on?' " [This is me again. Please note the excellent dialogue-proving question.] "That meeting led to a further meeting with the CEO, which eventually led us to the sale of the project proposed. We helped our client because we learned about the needs of his organization, and also brought a service that was valuable to the company.

"Probably our single largest challenge is showing our clients how value can be derived from a financial statement audit. When we succeed, we also achieve our goals of becoming business advisors to our clients. It may sound corny, but we *do* believe that success breeds success."

Thank you, Lars, for that testimonial about the importance of creating the right kind of atmosphere, taking advantage of situations, and asking the right questions. That's what this chapter is all about—how to ask questions to get customers to reveal information that no one else has, and how to create an atmosphere of complete disclosure through conversation that encourages the exchange of information at a more complex level.

Think again about the quarter-half-quarter model that we devoted so much time to in Chapter 3. Remember that the "half" portion of the model, once you complete the first quarter requirements, is where the major sales emphasis is focused and where you gather the information you need in order to present your solution. I cannot stress enough the importance of developing your questioning techniques, because without them you don't have a chance. So I intend to examine the questioning techniques every which way so that you can effectively use them to interest your customer in changing his current buying habits and thereby accomplish your objective. At this point, before we move on, let's summarize the consultative selling categories we've been discussing and review why these techniques are important to completing your task. You need to know three things:

1. How to distinguish yourself from the competition by the way you ask questions
2. How to tell the difference between a recital and a dialogue question
3. How to design advanced questions called dialogue probes and, most important, multilayered questions to uncover new information

Identifying Dialogue Questions

As salespeople, we've all been coached in the difference between open and closed questions. Everyone, except, perhaps, dear Professor Meredith Gall, has encouraged this method. It's also an approach used by those who make up tests, such as teachers and professors. But if you can't identify these questions, then you might use them when you shouldn't. So, as your high school English teacher would say, let's begin. (Do you hear the tap-tap-tap of her pencil against her podium? I do.) Open-ended questions typically begin with a *w*—*who, what, where, when,* and *why.* They're designed to coax the customer into responding freely and offering lots of information. Closed questions do just the opposite and seek yes or no answers, soliciting responses to choices or alternatives.

I always thought that using open and closed questions was the smartest way to sell my service, until I stumbled upon that article by Meredith Gall that I discussed in detail earlier in this chapter. Gall said that open and closed questions are only the beginning and that at best they can build a foundation. You should understand the role these questions usually play and focus on the types of questions that reveal more useful information—recital and, especially, dialogue questions.

Put in sports terms, recital questions are like tossing a football back and forth. That game can be satisfactory and fun for a while, but you don't end up scoring a touchdown. Similarly, these questions don't really stimulate the customer to think much and are pretty standard among salespeople. If you stick with recital questions, you'll find out facts, figures, and some details, which is not a means to an end but an opportunity to "warm up" the conversation. The downfall for too many sales-people is they tend to limit themselves to asking recital questions so that they don't move much beyond the twenty-yard line. Besides, that approach doesn't exactly help differentiate you from everyone else who uses it.

On the other hand, what you're looking for is increasingly detailed information that can engage your customer more in the sales process. These kinds of questions—what I call dialogue-probing questions—can stimulate expanded complex thinking because they involve more extensive conversation between you or your CSR and the customer and solicit not just correct answers but also new responses and new information. Remember how Lars Mawn of Deloitte & Touche explained earlier how he used dialogue-probing questions to engage his client, eventually winning a large engagement.

These questions can create comparisons that will stimulate new thoughts and, eventually, lead the customer to see a need for a change in her buying behavior, which is what you're ultimately looking for. They're a means to an end. You want her to buy your product or service instead of the competition's. Or, if the customer is already buying from you, you want to increase your penetration in the company for additional lines of products or services. You don't want to be viewed as just another vendor. Ideally, you'd like to assume the role of a partner, someone who truly understands the customer's business.

Remember, not only are you trying to alter the way your customer thinks of you; you're also focusing on how you can change your questioning approach so that you can be more effective. It doesn't really matter whether your questions are open or closed as much as it matters if they fall into the categories of recital or dialogue. Consider these examples of questions:

"What are your goals?"
"What have been your challenges?"

"Who are the decision makers?"
"How has your business been?"

What kinds of questions are these? If you said recital, give yourself a gold star. When you run into a friend or business associate, what's one of the first questions you ask? Is it "How's business"? Instead try something like, "How is the Fed's latest move affecting your business compared to others in your field?" Aside from having your friend look at you as if you've just returned from outer space, that question will certainly get what you're after—information.

Now, don't get me wrong. There's really nothing wrong with using recital questions. Remember that little exercise you did earlier on your most commonly asked questions? Even though most of them were recital, they still served the purpose of collecting information about the customer's business. But is that your sole objective? Obviously, I don't think so. So let me repeat one of our objectives here, sprinkled with a solid dose of reality. From the customer's point of view, you are the same as every other salesperson. He views your products and services, pricing, and after-market support as comparable to the competition's. And if he assumes all these issues to be the same, he also puts you in that "sameness" framework. So what's the major factor that you can truly change? You. You are capable of making or breaking a sale, of building a special relationship and distinguishing yourself from the competition.

The Dialogue-Probing Question—Your Best Tool

Now that you know why sticking with recital questions alone will not help you meet your sales goals, let's move on to a discussion of other, more productive questioning techniques that CSRs, as well as salespeople, can adopt. Let's go into more detail on dialogue-probing questions. There are three aspects to remember here: (1) Avoid using the five "W's"; (2) begin your questions with descriptive words; and, most important, (3) create a comparison. How do you do this? Pay close attention.

The classic five "w" questions—who, what, when, why, and

where—won't cut it here. Remember the way journalists ask questions. They tap their brains to come up with more descriptive questions that require answers beyond a simple yes or no response. Words like "describe," "explore," "explain," and "share with me" come to mind. These words allow you break away from your "w" questioning mold, open up the customer, and generate a more in-depth response. Any phrase like "could you share with me" or "would you tell me" can also work.

Let's focus more on how to create a comparison with your dialogue-probing questions. Comparisons are designed to lead customers to evaluate their current status against their status at some other time. These comparisons could involve factors such as changes over time, industry trends, market trends, or surveys and reports (Figure 5-3). By adding the dynamic of a comparison, you expand the way a person thinks and responds. As the revered poet and writer Ralph Waldo Emerson once said, "If you can stretch a man's mind, you own it." I believe Emerson would concur with our objective of trying to generate new customer responses while moving away from recital or rote answers in order to glean more information than our competitors. This is especially important in today's selling environment, where there's so much similarity among products and services.

Are you ready for some examples of how you can alter your "w" question into a dialogue-probing one? Let's start with the two questions that are probably on everyone's list: goals and challenges. Look back at the four recital questions we gave as examples earlier, and let's rewrite them into dialogue-probing questions:

Figure 5-3.   Elements of comparison.

Factor	Sample Elements
Time	Past, present, future
Data	Reports, surveys, studies
Market Conditions	Industry trends, cultural issues

Recital	Dialogue-Probing
1a. What are your goals? (time)	Describe for me your goals and how they compare to your thoughts of a year ago. Describe for me your goals and the course of events that led to their identification.
1b. What are your goals? (trend)	Tell me about your goals and how they compare with those of others in your industry.
2. What are your challenges? (marketplace)	Tell me about the challenges you experience with your department and how they compare with those of others you talk to in the industry.
3. Who are the decision makers? (time)	Could you tell me who your raw material decision makers are today compared with recent years when your company relied on only one supplier?
4. How has your business been? (survey)	I recently saw a study in *The Wall Street Journal* about the price increase for raw materials. Could you share with me what you are experiencing compared to the article's findings?

As you can tell, the familiar "what are your goals?" question can be retooled with the time element added to it: "Describe for me your goals and how they compare to your thoughts of a year ago," or "Describe for me your goals and the course of events that led to their identification." If you want to add the element of a trend comparison to the goal question, try "Tell me about your goals and how they compare with those of others in your marketplace." Let's try a "what are your challenges" revision. How about adding the marketplace element to come up with, "Tell me about the challenges you experience with your department and how they compare with those of others you talk to in the industry"? A survey question could sound like, "I recently saw a study in *The Wall Street Journal* about the price increase for raw materials. Could you share with me your experience compared to the survey's findings?

This is a lot of information to digest, so the following is a little test that can help determine if you're on the right track. So, here we go with another little test. I hope that your pencil is still sharpened.

Select one of the following options to change the recital questions to dialogue-probing questions.

1. How does our proposal meet your needs?
    a. What was your reaction after reading our proposal, and how well does it meet your needs?
    b. After reviewing our proposal, tell me your thoughts about how our ideas address your issues compared with your other options.
    c. Of all of the proposals you're reviewing, where are we positioned?
2. How is the economy affecting your business?
    a. Knowing the concerns about our present economy, share with me the economy's impact on your business and how it compares with prior years.
    b. The economy is affecting many businesses. How it is affecting yours?
    c. Managing a business in today's economy is difficult. How is it going for you?
3. What's your business strategy?
    a. What difficulties are you experiencing in growing your business?
    b. How have your business strategies changed over the years?
    c. Describe for me your business strategy and the course of events that led to its development.
    d. How do you determine your business strategy?

Now grade yourself. The correct response for question number 1 is b, for question 2, a, and for question number 3, c.

How'd you do? (A trick question in recital form. Did you

catch it?) Give yourself another gold star even if you got only one question correct, because that means you're on the right track and understand the difference between the less effective recital question and the more productive dialogue-probing question. As you can tell, the key is only a few simple words— "share with me," "compare with," "describe," and "tell me." If you remember just those words and make sure you use them, you'll find yourself asking a dialogue-probing question.

Distinguishing the Serious Customer— Action Steps

Now that you're learning how to fashion the right kinds of questions in order to acquire the information you need to change your customer's buying habits, it's a good idea to adopt another concept that is part of the "half" stage of the quarter-half-quarter model. Known as action steps, these moves support your questioning techniques, help save you time in the process, and organize your approach, as well as teach you how to distinguish a seemingly interested customer from one who only appears interested. Personally, I like to think of this as a prioritization method. I define action steps as collecting a "buy-in" and mutual collaboration from the customer, who has taken an action using his own time and resources that will meet your objectives; in other words, he has taken some kind of purposeful action that makes it seem as if he's interested in buying your product or service. Those actions could be:

- Completing a questionnaire
- Traveling to your facility for a tour
- Arranging a meeting at the customer's location and inviting others to attend
- Sharing costs
- Calling references

Sounds really positive, doesn't it? You can almost feel that commission in your hands now. But I wouldn't go out and spend it quite yet, because this is another customer technique that can blow your sale. Let's try another test here:

Determine which of the following are action steps:

Completes and returns a questionnaire
Brings others along to join you for lunch
Requests a proposal
Calls references
Attends a seminar hosted at your facility
Asks you to forward literature
Calls you back
Evaluates your product
Writes a recommendation
Gives you an opportunity to bid

Do you think you marked the correct action steps? The correct actions are "completes and returns a questionnaire," "calls references," "attends a seminar hosted at your facility," and "writes a recommendation." Why are the others wrong? Because an action step requires activity by both the CSR and the customer; the customer must make a move that uses his own time and resources, too, not just yours. Perhaps a couple of examples will explain it more fully.

Action Steps in Action

Let's say a CSR receives a phone call in the mid-afternoon from a customer asking, "Can you help me?" He says he needs to present the CSR's proposal to his committee, and he needs to have it in his hands by the next morning. Now think about what he's telling the CSR. He isn't exhibiting a need or indicating any action on his part. He's just called out of the blue because he's just left a meeting and he needs to make the proposal quickly, so he says. So what does the CSR do? Well, probably what most CSRs (or most any other salesperson, for that matter) would do—work late in order to complete the proposal and send it overnight to the customer.

Then, the next morning the CSR calls the customer's office, but he's in a meeting. He doesn't call back, so she calls again and is told she just missed him. Hmmm. But she's still really excited about the prospect of a sale (and perhaps a bit tired); after all, the customer had called and asked for the proposal. She finally gets him on the phone late that afternoon and eagerly asks him, "Well, what do you think?" He responds, "I'm sorry. I haven't had a chance to look at it yet." Brother, what a disappointment! He sure did need it right away, didn't he? The CSR is furious, but she maintains her cool and asks him to give her a call after he's had a chance to read it and maybe let her know when he thinks that might be. End of story, end of quick sale. Beginning of aggravation and learning process.

Could the CSR have taken her time in preparing the proposal? Probably. Did she have to get it in the overnight mail, or could she have simply dropped it in the regular mail delivery? Regular mail would have been fine. Why? Because he never gave her that all-important indication that he was ready to make a commitment to change. Requesting a proposal ASAP doesn't fulfill that requirement.

Action steps require the customer to do something for the CSR. In this case, however, the already overworked CSR was asked to do a lot more. In fact, she was so busy that she might not have given it her best effort, anyway, and she's losing control.

Let me give you another example, one that happened to me not that long ago. A company in Cleveland called saying it was desperate to have me come out and teach a sales training course as quickly as possible. How soon could I be there? As is my standard operating procedure, I asked the caller to fill out a brief questionnaire on the company, its needs, challenges, and important issues. He said, "No problem." (I've learned over the years to be real skeptical when someone tells me "no problem.") He agreed to fill out the questionnaire immediately (we offered to fax it to him) and return it to us that afternoon. Well, you can probably guess what happened. The questionnaire didn't come back that afternoon or several weeks later. He never returned my phone calls, either.

I love to relate that story because for the past several months I've given several seminars for this company. When the sales training manager finally contacted me again, he was terribly embarrassed and sent all the materials to me (including the questionnaire) in the overnight mail.

Here's another variation on that same theme (I've got a million of them). A major Philadelphia insurance company contacted us last year inquiring about our training seminars. It filled out the questionnaire and sent it back promptly, noting that the program sounded exactly like what its people needed. However, management wanted to see the program in action. My sales associate, misunderstanding the company's intentions, asked how many people it wanted to enroll in the next session. The manager promptly corrected her. Because the company was a potential customer, management thought it was perfectly OK to insist on seeing a seminar first, at no cost, before enrolling. As a counteroffer I suggested that its department head attend a brief breakfast seminar that was planned for the following week as my guest, but his other two people would have to pay for the seminar. The company still insisted that all three should see a full seminar for free. You can guess what I told them—politely, of course. And, no, I never heard from them again. I really feel sorry for all my competitors, whom they must have hit up with the same request, too. (P.S. They never hired a training vendor.)

Because I want to force these unsolicited phone callers to give me a true indication of their intent, the action step I've adopted is simple. This questionnaire I've referred to is my action step—my screening device. With this, I'm requiring them to do something for me before I make a move. This is how it works in action. Recently a company official requested information on my seminars. I told him about the questionnaire, so he asked me to forward one in the overnight mail. I asked him to give me his overnight mail account number. After all, shouldn't he pay for it? He hesitated a moment, and then gave me his account number. Obviously, this is no guarantee that he's going to follow through enrolling in a seminar, but at least he gave me an indication of his intentions. Fortunately, this customer ended up enrolling in a seminar. I've always wondered whether he made the connection to my request when we discussed action steps during the seminar.

Keeping Control of the Process

As CSRs, I know that you're used to some kind of departmental signal that lets you know when a call is waiting. Earlier I referred to a type of ticker tape that one company used. Many others use blinking red lights. So here you are; the red light is blinking, and you've got a guy on the phone making outrageous requests for information that will probably never result in any kind of sale. Consider those requests desk clutter. You're too busy answering the phones and moving through the consultative selling model to bother with someone who is not willing to help you meet your objectives. Pushing papers doesn't produce results, and I know you won't get compensated for the number of proposals you prepare and send out. Your time is too valuable. I realize that as a CSR it's tough to just terminate the contact. You might not feel you have that authority. Besides, that person is a customer of yours, and you don't want to anger him so that he runs to your competition. On the other hand, it doesn't make sense to waste your time on customers who give no indication that they are willing to make a commitment to change.

But sales managers can help their CSRs succeed. Remember, a CSR is geared toward helping customers, and the strategy of transforming CSRs into an inside sales team offers them a new opportunity to strut their stuff. It can be exciting to encounter a new set of challenges. However, they know, and managers should know, that if they're spending too much time on one customer, then they're not getting to the other customer who's causing that red light to blink madly. It's already a challenge for CSRs to keep their phone calls short. Even though the whole process of calling for an action step should take no more than two minutes, most new CSRs will initially take longer to accomplish it. So let's look again at action steps from another perspective.

Action steps can be used to prioritize the activities of the day. Maybe five customers have asked for more information. The CSR may choose to work late to complete the project, even though no overtime is paid. But the action steps can help him decide which requests should be handled first and which can be saved for the next day. Here's an example. Once I got a call from an Ohio company manager expressing interest in my seminars. When I suggested that she fill out the questionnaire, she said she had to be in the Philadelphia area (an hour away from my office) the following week and asked if she could come by. I invited her for breakfast, and I'll be darned if she didn't drive an extra hour to visit with me. Breakfast was good, though. And I certainly did put on a seminar for her company.

There are a number of action steps you can create to organize your time as well as weed out the really not interested customers. The need to fill out a questionnaire works well to separate the bona fide buyers and the tire kickers. I recommend using such a form if you don't already. Suggest that the customer call some of your other customers who use the product, or visit your office to see it in action. Try evaluating the customer's statements along the lines we discussed earlier—is he negative, noncommittal, or positive when you ask him to do something for you? Listen carefully, because, although it's gratifying to hear excitement in your customer's voice, you really can't assume he's sincere without some indication of action on his part. If it's not there, just put that request on the back burner—way back.

I can hear your CSRs now. "They're my customers. I could never do that to them. Besides, they're such nice people." Maybe so, but they're not doing anything for you so that you can be productive and make some money. Every day customers want you to jump through hoops for them. They want their orders filled yesterday. You've been there. You've dealt with it. You need to get over any worries about upsetting your client when you're making legitimate demands. They certainly don't worry about upsetting you with their outrageous requests. Besides, everyone is busy, so it may not make much difference if you have to put him off for a couple of days.

Losing the Deal

What's the moral of this particular set of stories? "We don't know what his intentions are until we clarify them with a series of action steps." When he says to you, "This sounds good, but I have to bring it to committee," what he's actually doing is setting the hook for another customer-action known as futuring (we'll get to that concept a bit later). So how might your action step respond to this customer statement? Try, "Why not have your assistant send a memo to others in your company recommending my product?" That forces him to make a commitment to you.

Go back to that original list of common customer comments that you wrote down in Chapter 4 to borrow some questions that you can use on your action step questionnaire. Not only can these serve as action steps; a completed questionnaire may contain information about the customer that your competition doesn't have. In sales terms, the customer becomes a qualified customer. Perhaps she won't buy *from you,* but she will buy. I wrote an article in a Philadelphia business journal that suggested 50 percent of all customers won't swing at what you pitch, so the trick is to identify who that other 50 percent are. Even a batting average of .300 or .400 is considered outstanding, and could get you into the Hall of Fame.

Losing a deal—and you will lose deals, even if you follow the program to the letter—may only mean you've been outsold. And I believe it's better to lose the contract than to have the negotiations hang open over your head and waste your time. The skills will get you efficiently through the sales process, but you may be unable to close the sale due to other circumstances that you can't possibly control.

A Practice Exercise

While you are employing action steps, you're adding another element that will help you accomplish the same objectives as dialogue-probing questions—uncovering your customer's needs. As we've discussed, these questions differ dramatically from the standard sales questions that your customer hears. In fact, if he wanted to save himself some time he could probably just pre-record his answers to and play the tape for each salesperson. These are questions like:

"What are your problems?"
"What keeps you up at night?"
[*for selling a cellular phone*] "Where do you make most of
   your calls? Whom do you call the most?"

That last question isn't bad because it is asking for more specific
information, but it's not all that different from the questions the
customer hears all the time. Instead, it's easier to remember to
begin your questions with phrases such as "In the event of . . . ,"
or "All things being equal . . . ," which will help break questioning patterns—and grab the attention of your customer.

   It's time for another test to see how well you can write dialogue questions. For the first question, refer back to your original list of ten recital and dialogue questions. Pick one or two
recital/informational questions and change them to dialogue-
probing questions. Begin with a descriptive word or phrase, and
end with a comparison. The following questions can act as
guidelines for this exercise:

   "Describe for me what you think about at night compared to years ago."

   "Tell me about your goals and how they've evolved
   [are you a decision maker?]"

   "Explain to me your selection process and how it compares with the process for other projects of the same
   size."

Here's a list of words and phrases you can use:

   Describe
   Explore
   Explain
   Tell me
   In the event of
   Share with me
   On the basis of
   Please go into more detail

When you draft your questions, some of you will not use the word "describe" but will use your own version. That's terrific, but be sure to use a conversational tone. Don't forget to use "compare" or "contrast" to make sure you get a comparison. Many professional interviewers use comparisons to create an effective question. For example, on election night in 1996 I watched Maria Shriver interview George Stephanopoulos, President Clinton's aide. At one point she asked him, "On a personal note, tell me how this evening compares to four years ago." It was a good question, and it elicited a rather lengthy answer from Stephanopoulos. To maintain my nonpartisanship, I also watched some of the 1996 Republican convention, where there was very little news for the reporters to discuss. Instead, the reporters took to making comparisons to try to create a story.

The sales training manager at the international corporation who told his CSR transitional story in Chapter 4 made a particularly good point to me when he noted that he wanted to teach his people how to get the one nugget of information that no one else [no competitor] has. A well-thought-out dialogue-probing question can do that for you. But don't get carried away with yourself; "How are you?" doesn't need to be revised to be "Please tell me how you are compared to yesterday." Just use your common sense.

Having relayed nearly everything I can tell you about creating dialogue-probing questions, I'd like you to create your own. For the first one, revise one of your recital questions. For the second, completely create a new question. Take your time.

1. Change one recital question into one dialogue-probing question.
2. Draft your own personal (business) dialogue-probing question.

Recital Question to Dialogue-Probing:

_____

_____

_____

_____

Dialogue-Probing Question:

_____

_____

_____

_____

_____

I'm going to assume that you started your dialogue-probing questions with "describe" and ended with a time comparison. That was a good technique to use. Now try it again, this time starting with a different word or phrase and ending with a comparison.

_____

_____

How'd you do? Let me give you a sample question that you could have used. "Tell me about your goals, and how they compare with what industry analysts are suggesting."

Why am I putting you through this? There's a common business cliché that says that in order to encourage employees to make significant changes in their work approach, you need to get your people to "move way out of their box." And I want to "unbox" you from your standard CSR approach. You know that this strategy makes sense, but you may be saying to yourself, "How can I do this? My customers have never heard these kinds of questions out of me before. I've never asked such a long question. I'm worried my customer won't accept these questions."

Bet you didn't know I could read minds. But let me respond to your concerns. It's not important whether or not the customer will accept these questions. Once you get comfortable asking them, your customer will answer them.

Now that you understand recital and dialogue-probing questioning techniques, our next mission is to decipher, in detail, the concept of multilayered probing questions (MLPQs), a questioning technique that has been used by salespeople for several years and has proved its usefulness time and again in helping to create a thought-provoking sales discussion with the customer. Even if you forget everything else I've discussed so far, be sure to pay close attention here, because this strategy is really the guts of the proper questioning system, and it can make a significant difference in your sales success rate. And if you thought dialogue-probing questions could be long, just wait until you get a look at typical MLPQs. As the vaudeville performers used to say, "You ain't seen nothing yet."

6

"These Questions Seem So Long. Won't My Client Fall Asleep?"

The Concept of Multilayered Probing Questions

What's your favorite type of casserole? My friend makes one that his grandmother always made when he was a child; now he makes it for his kids. It's called "glop." If I recall correctly, that's what his little brother called it when he was young, and at this point no one really remembers the real name, so everyone just calls it glop. It sounds awful, but it's really good because it contains some of my favorite foods—tomatoes, sweet peppers, ground beef, pasta (penne or ziti), covered with melted mozzarella cheese. He mixes it all together in a casserole dish and bakes it in the oven until it's steaming. With a hunk of Italian bread, it's great.

So why am I giving you a recipe? Because that's an appetizing way to explain multilayered probing questions, which can be intimidating just because of the name. But the name actually describes what it is. Like our delectable layered casserole, MLPQs contain three layers of answers and questions. Perhaps most important, they combine all our question types. When you put dialogue-probing, informational, and layered questions together, along with a sprinkling of recital questions and related techniques, you get a mixture of questions that will help achieve your goal of creating a stimulating, thought-provoking discussion. Done successfully, it will also move you one step closer to closing the sale. Even though they are three-part questions—statement of fact, observation, and dialogue—MLPQs can be executed in just twelve to fifteen seconds. Remember your original ten questions? Some can be answered on the questionnaire; one or two can be changed to dialogue-probes. In every conversation, however, to bridge to a new product, a new topic, or a new issue, simply use a good MLPQ (Figure 6-1).

MLPQs help you better understand the customer's exact thoughts because they direct your customer to reflect on the situation; establish comparisons; talk about the past, present, and future implications and conditions; and assist the customer in drawing a conclusion based on existing and new information provided by you. Clearly, this process is designed to move your customer conversation to a more advanced level, help you generate that in-depth conversation we've been talking about, and get to the point of a stronger relationship to help you close the sale. This is a strategy that seasoned salespeople, as well as novice CSRs, can certainly relate to.

Creating MLPQs

Every day, people are asked to compare their experiences with those of others concerning important events. For example, how

Figure 6-1.   MLPQ as a bridge for a new product, topic, or issue.

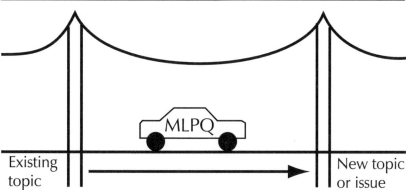

many times have people asked you, "Do you know where you were when John F. Kennedy was shot, Neil Armstrong walked on the moon, the Challenger exploded, Woodstock 'happened,' Bill Clinton was first elected to the presidency, O.J. Simpson was found not guilty of murder in his criminal trial yet liable for the murders during the civil trial, your favorite old-line department store was changing its name?" When you found out about these events, probably from the newspapers or TV news, you wanted to know more about them. Maybe you talked to a friend, asking, "Did you hear on the news, see today's paper, or hear on the radio that . . . ," and you explain what you're talking about, reciting the information. After you heard the O.J. Simpson verdicts, while talking to your friends, you probably gave an opinion one way or another, then asked your friends, "So what do you think? What's your opinion?"

You ask MLPQ questions every day, and you don't even realize it. We get our information about what's going on in our world, country, state, town and neighborhood, and school district from third-party sources—TV, radio, newspapers, rumor, and office gossip. That same conversational process that we're comfortable with in personal life that generates communication and information is what we want to use in our business dealings to help our budding CSRs effectively bridge conversations from reactive to proactive. You want these critically important MLPQs to have a conversational tone, too, to be most effective. Did you ever think that office gossip could act as a template for making sales calls? The next time you're chatting with your coworkers at the coffee machine, pay close attention to how they relay information to you. Do you hear the MLPQs?

To aid in your understanding, let me briefly sketch the major elements of MLPQs before I go into more depth:

The Three Parts of MLPQs

1. Statement of fact
2. Observation (optional)
3. Probing question

Four Design Prerequisites You Need to Follow When Creating MLPQs

1. Fact must address an issue of concern for the customer.
2. Facts cannot be challenged.

3. Facts must come from a credible source.
4. Refrain from mentioning your own company name or data.

Let's look at the three parts of the MLPQ—the statement of fact, the observation, and the probing question. Your job is to use this outline to help you create your questions, and even go through a couple of dry runs until you feel comfortable with them. So get a pencil.

The Statement of Fact

The statement of fact is critical because it allows you to lure the customer into an in-depth dialogue. Use the four-question design criteria or prerequisites just given to win over your customer. First, address a key issue that concerns your customer. Depending on the circumstances, this key issue might be innovation, technology, safety, financial markets, productivity, or efficiency. Let's say, for example, you know from previous conversations with your customer that he's particularly concerned with safety issues, such as the risk facing people who work late and must walk through dark parking lots, rising insurance costs associated with safety problems, employee psychological problems, and the growing regard among companies. So read several articles on the issue (remember, you can tap into your company's databases after regular business hours, or check the library), and become conversant on the topic.

To apply the MLPQ "safety issue" topic, start the conversation with the following:

You: Do you receive *The Wall Street Journal?*
Customer response: Yes.
You: Did you happen to see the recent article about employee safety and the rising costs of insurance associated with claims?
Customer response: No, I didn't read that particular article.
You: Well, the article discussed how many companies are using alternative methods of training and prevention to improve safety and lower costs. I was wondering . . . describe what is happening at your company. How does it compare to what the article suggests?

After citing these problems—"I was reading an article the other day about how a growing number of companies are concerned about safety issues. They worry about . . . I was wondering, what's been your experience? How does it compare to the article findings?" There you have it, an MLPQ based on an article, just as you would discuss and question a friend about a news event. But in this case, you've probably succeeded in triggering concerns about safety issues with your customer (and you probably sell some kind of safety device or service). This is what I like to call setting the hook. The challenge to this task is to become comfortable with the concept and the topic so that you can ask your questions in a conversational tone.

Second, the question or statement should be so factual and in tune with current issues that it cannot be challenged by the customer. You should sound so well informed that it won't even occur to the customer that you may not completely understand the subject. To him, you're brilliant.

Third, your facts should originate in a credible source, such as *The Wall Street Journal,* trade publications, surveys, or studies. Remember earlier we talked about using your company's computerized resources, such as the Internet? That's where you'll find your credible sources, and so much more. However, now I'll turn around and say that there are times when you don't necessarily need a credible source, such as a newspaper or magazine article—but that's for specialized situations only. (If the issue is common to an industry and is covered by governmental regulations, a specific source is not necessary. Sample topics include auto airbags, carbon dioxide detectors, lead paint removal, all cancer-causing agents, and most workplace issues. Each industry has its own cross to bear, and even though it would be nice to have a documented fact, these and other regulated issues are still readily accepted.) Because it will take you some research time to dig up your facts, I suggest you research no more than five issues, regardless of how many customers you have to approach. After all, the customers probably won't be talking to each other, so you can repeat your questions.

One more point here. If your product or service appeals to a broad geographic or industrial audience, don't try to cover every issue your product can solve. Just focus on a few categories, and be specific with those.

The fourth criterion for creating a statement of fact concerns what you should not do. Don't use information you've gleaned from your company or even talk about your company. This may sound counterproductive, but consider this. If the fact comes from your company, the customer might believe the information is tainted or skewed, which could detract from your credibility and focus attention on your product and selling intention before you're ready. Besides, should the customer disagree with your statement, then technically he's disagreeing with you, which can damage your relationship. Remember, an important part of this process is to build your relationship; don't take the chance of doing anything that could undo what you've already accomplished.

The Observation

Now let's move on to the second part of the MLPQ—the observation. This element can play a dual role in your questioning technique. It can help support your statement of fact by lending credibility ("Many feel that way"), or it can give a contrary perspective that can provoke an alternative point of view ("The *Journal* said this, but the *Times* said that"). In either case, you can use this element to your advantage by either strengthening your viewpoint or contradicting the fact under discussion. This technique can lead your customer in either direction and still help build your relationship. Most important, this step is optional, so use it only if it makes sense to do so. For example, should you have a fence sitter, this is a good technique to use to push him off the fence.

The Probing Question

This leads us to the final part of the MLPQ—the probing question. This part asks the customer what he is experiencing and how it compares with what you discussed in the earlier "fact" stage. For example, if your fact stemmed from an article in *The Wall Street Journal*, your question could be, "Describe for me your experience with this issue and how your experience compares with the point of view of the article." Phrase it like that when the fact and observation are in agreement. But if the fact and observation contradict each other, change the probing question to "Describe for me your experience and how it compares to what appear to be two diverse opinions."

However you word probing questions, they must be "safe" and not include a kicker at the end (e.g., "don't you agree?"), because you'll end up with a yes or no answer. (People tend to answer the last part of multiple questions.) If you're using a "what is your experience" question, it must tie in with the fact and observation of the customer's everyday life. You really have to understand probe questions before you can create a well-done MLPQ, so if you still have some concerns, please review the previous chapter on dialogue-probing questions.

While we're at it, don't forget that MLPQs can contain all the types of questions we've already discussed (e.g., informational), as well as a few others we really haven't delved into yet. But trust me, I'll be kind in this chapter.

Now comes an exercise. I want you to identify the following questions as either "I" for informational, "P" for dialogue-probing, or MLPQ for multilayered probing.

1. ___ What's your budget for this project?
2. ___ Describe the circumstances and the course of events that led to the current condition.
3. ___ How many employees do you have?
4. ___ Recent surveys indicated a need to improve productivity. This was supported by several leading business experts. Tell me your experience. How does it compare with what the survey says?
5. ___ Describe your biggest challenge.
6. ___ Describe your biggest challenge. How does it compare with the experience of other industry leaders?
7. ___ We've been getting a lot of calls on the proposed new health care policy. Because the policy calls for higher rates and reduced coverage, many organizations are looking for alternatives. Tell me your perspective on the package and how this compares with your situation.

8. ___ Top economists are noticing a reduction in customer spending. Recent reports state that the opposite is true. Describe your position and how it compares to what seems to be two diverse opinions.
9. ___ Who is your current vendor?
10. ___ Explain the selection process of a new supplier at your company. How does it compare with your previous selection process?

How difficult was that? I know that some questions were pretty obvious, but others may have gone one way or another, so let's evaluate some of them. Question 1 was pretty obvious. It's an information question in a recital format, as are questions 3, 5, and 9. Question 5 requires a bit more discussion, so I'll come back to it in a minute. Question 2 is obviously a probing question because it begins with a phrase and asks the customer what he's experiencing. Question 4 is a MLPQ because it makes a statement of fact by addressing a key issue that concerns the customer (survey; need to improve productivity), comes from a credible source (leading business experts), and is followed by a dialogue-probing question (begins with "Tell me . . .").

Question 6 is a dialogue-probing question because it begins with a phrase and ends with a comparison question. Question 7 is an MLPQ because, for starters, it's so darn long. Also, it incorporates all the design criteria for a statement of fact—it addresses a key issue of concern to customer, it cannot be challenged (the CSR notes that many people have been copying the newspaper story and distributing it around their offices, which automatically instills the notion of change), and it ends with a probing question. "Organizations are looking for alternatives" satisfies the "credible source" prerequisite as well as making an observation, and the final part ("Tell me . . .") is clearly a dialogue-probing question. I realize this question might push your "it's so long" button, but it really only takes a few seconds, because one sentence naturally flows into the next. Try timing it yourself if you don't believe me. Besides, if your customer really is interested in this issue, it won't seem long to him at all.

Question 8 is also an MLPQ for reasons similar to those for question 7, but this one's observations present two differing points of view—a reduction in customer spending or an increase in customer spending. Stating opposing points of view is an effective way of stimulating conversation with the customer. That's an observation. Question 9 is, again, an obvious informational recital question. It's also terribly self-serving, as is question one, so try to avoid those kinds of questions. You can find out that information elsewhere, perhaps from the customer's assistant. Question 2 is a dialogue-probing question because it begins with a phrase and ends with a comparison question.

Now, let's return to question 5, the informational question. This is categorized as an informational question, even though it is identical to the first part of question 6, a probing question, because it uses only an opening phrase and doesn't include the necessary comparison component as question 6 does.

Additional Hints on Creating MLPQs

Do you feel somewhat proficient now at composing and asking MLPQs yet? No? Then, to aid your learning process, check out this list of characteristics you should consider when designing your MLPQ:

- Be clear and concise.
- Elicit a thought before a customer can formulate a response.
- Require the customer to evaluate the new information or concepts and compare them to life experiences.
- Generate a response that the customer has not thought about before.
- Relate directly to the customer's current work situation.
- Know what ideas you are developing before you compose the question (don't just make up the questions—the customer will be able to figure that out).
- Relate directly to the customer's objectives and achievements with minimal direction from you.
- Turn the spotlight on the customer.
- When speaking to more than one person, phrase the question to everyone to let the burden of thought fall on everyone.

- Be prepared to listen and respond with additional questions.
- Do not think of your next question. Listen.
- Require focused thought and continuing effort to make a response.
- Always take notes.

Need a little bit more help? Review these sample questions and additional hints to help solidify the major points you need to remember:

- When your fact or issue and your observation are in agreement, I recommend using the following probe question:
"Describe for me your experience in this area. How does it compare with the xxxxxxxx?"
- When your fact and observation contradict each other, I suggest using the following probe question:
"Describe for me your experience in this area. How does it compare with what seems to be two diverse opinions?"

Because the MLPQ is the backbone for this entire sales approach that CSRs need to learn, I'll try to reinforce the primary principles for this questioning technique by reviewing some of the key points and offering some additional hints and approaches to help you make the best of your MLPQs.

When creating your multilayered question, read it out loud and time it. If it seems too long or too choppy, then it probably is. You can either shorten the question to ten to fifteen seconds, make it more conventional, or simply drop the "observation" section, if appropriate. If you choose to simply shorten it, substitute the word "because" when asking your observation question (e.g., "Companies are looking to reduce costs. Because of this, they're seeking alternative methods"), because it ties the thoughts together and helps validate what you're talking about. It also gives an indication that change is taking place and that there's a reason for it.

The alternative choice—making the question more conversational—involves simply talking through the question to the customer. For example, you might start the question by saying, "The other day I was reading an article in the *Journal*—I think it was last week. In any event, the article focused on how companies are looking to reduce costs. Did you happen to see that article? It talked about. . . ." By starting the question this way, the customer is initially unaware that you are asking a question or setting up a question. This kind of question is masked by the conversational tone and resembles the normal course of conversation. Personally, I prefer this kind of questioning technique because it tends to simplify the process, puts both the customer and the salesperson (or CSR) at ease, and makes for a smoother discussion.

One of my favorite stories about MLPQs concerns one of those call-in radio talk shows where listeners call in, give their first names only and where they live, and then ask a question of the host or guest. A while back, when I was on a business trip to New York to give a speech, my hotel room radio was turned to a local sports call-in show. The topic was NFL quarterbacks; callers were comparing their skills, and so on. At that moment they were discussing a particular quarterback who was not playing up to par. A young man called in and said his name was Tony from Brooklyn. In a thick Brooklyn accent, he asked, "Two years ago *Sports Illustrated* said this guy was the ultimate weapon. Today's paper said he wasn't too good. Why don't you guys tell us your opinions compared to these articles?"

My ears perked up. Tony had just asked a multilayered probing question! If Tony from Brooklyn, without training, can ask an MLPQ in an everyday kind of conversation, so can anyone else, including CSRs.

Another strategy is to reduce the question to only two parts—the statement of fact and the probing question, eliminating the observation section entirely. As I mention earlier, the observation is optional if you don't seem to need it. Dropping the observation works well if you believe the customer is truly limited by time or if the selling environment is disturbed by distractions so that his ability to concentrate is impaired—maybe he has to get to a meeting, or someone has just shoved a report under his nose. Just move right from the statement of fact to the probing questions. If you practice this approach, it can still engage your customer in conversation.

Creating and Revising the MLPQ

It's time once again to practice what you've learned. I want you to draft your own MLPQ using an issue of concern for one of your customers. Feel free to look back at the hints and examples I gave your earlier, especially that template that begins "Describe for me your experiences. . . ." Don't worry about the length right now; if it does turn out to be too long, we'll go back and edit it along the lines we've already discussed.

MLPQ Draft 1

Fact:_____

_____

_____

_____

Observation:_____

_____

_____

_____

Probe:_____

_____

_____

_____

REVISION

> Fact:_____
>
> _____
>
> Observation:_____
>
> _____
>
> Probe:_____
>
> _____

How did you do? Too long? Then drop the observation. In your second editing attempt on the original question, instead of using the observation in an opposing or supportive role, why not reintroduce it by saying your version of "many companies are looking for alternatives because. . . ." Remember our "because" lesson in Chapter 4, when the student kept moving to the front of the copying machine line. He was most successful when he said he needed to use the machine "because I'm late for my class." "Because" is a positive word and gives a reason for your actions.

If you need to edit your MLPQ a third time, make it conversational. Remember, you're talking to the customer like a friend. And as the listener, the customer doesn't hear what you're saying as a three-part question. It's just a conversation, and you're following a model, or template, that just happens to end with a question. Besides, as I said earlier, I just think it's more comfortable to ask MLPQs in a conversational tone.

As you've probably noticing, the editing I've been leading you though is not the traditional kind of editing you may have used before. The editing doesn't necessarily make the question shorter, but it makes it better. In reality, you're creating a longer question, but the issue here is not the length as much as your and your customer's comfort level. While talking to your customer, you probably have fifteen seconds to ask a question, so instead of asking five informational questions, which net you basic information that doesn't really go anywhere, you have time to ask one really good MLPQ, from which you'll end up gaining more information.

Listening to Your Customers

Now that you've become expert at advanced questioning techniques, we need to look at the other side of the equation—listening. This is a vital component in every relationship—with your boss, your spouse, your coach, your in-laws, and on and on. My objective here is reinforce the importance of listening skills as you continue your quest to build a strong relationship and accurately access what your customer is saying. Asking questions helps distinguish you from your competition, but carefully listening to the responses can help you persuade your customer to relate more information pertinent to your question. By listening carefully, you are encouraging your customer to reveal more information about what he just explained. That allows you to create a need for change in the customer's way of thinking, which is crucial to moving toward closing the sale.

Think about this. As a salesperson, I'm sure you've been told during your career to uncover the customer's needs; then you're set to present your product/service as a solution. Certainly, this seems to make sense, but if we dig deeper, we find that this concept really falls apart. For example, let me ask you how many times you've uncovered your customer's needs, only to have him bid you good-bye with a handshake and a smile without committing to a sale? More often than you'd like to remember, right? So what went wrong? You determined the customer's needs, provided a great solution, and maybe even lowered your price to make your solution more attractive. The problem? Your customer did not see the need for change.

Think back to the quarter-half-quarter model I described in Chapter 3 (Figure 6-2). It reflects the three factors you're selling—a relationship, a need for change, and a solution. Too many salespeople and CSRs might be eager to move to the last quarter and offer a solution at this point. But you really should stay in the "half" section of the model because you're still gathering

Figure 6-2.   The quarter-half-quarter model for placing a sales call.

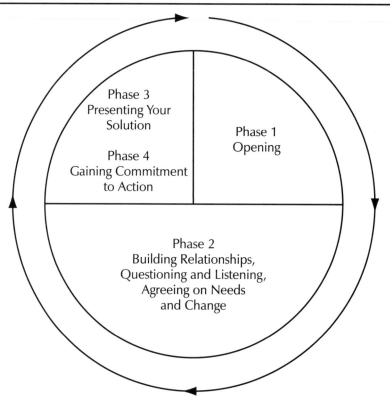

information, and customers typically don't purchase the product at this level.

The Three Levels of Customer Interest

How do you overcome customer inertia? You need to set the stage for change by determining the customer's interest first. A customer can fall into one of three categories of interest—Level 1, known as Opportunity; Level 2, known as Need; and Level 3, called Recognition for Change (Figure 6-3). Knowing the level of interest will lead to motivating your customer to consider a change in attitude toward you and your product. From there, you can convince your customer to recognize the need for change. Bear in mind that the customer's level of interest is what

Figure 6-3.   Levels of interest.

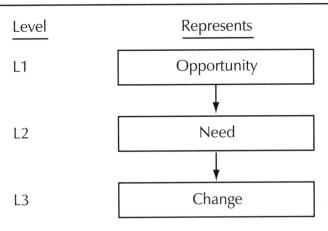

Level	Represents
L1	Opportunity
L2	Need
L3	Change

determines whether the sales process will continue to the next step.

At this point, it should be becoming clear to you why determining your customer's level of interest can also tell you his receptivity to change and whether the process will continue to the next step. Determining the customer's interest is the focus of the initial sales process.

Let's examine the three levels of interest more closely to see how they help you push your customer to recognize his need for change. Level 1, or L1, Opportunity, is where the customer recognizes the opportunity to correct an unsatisfactory situation; Level 2, or L2, Need, reflects a desire to address the unsatisfactory situation; and Level 3, or L3, Recognition for Change, is the level at which the customer faces the consequences of inaction. L1 is defined as revealing the customer's indication of areas in which your services can be positioned as a solution. However, opportunity differs from change and need in that it lacks a clear statement of desire to correct the situation at hand. For example, a statement such as "We have been thinking about talking to a vendor to improve product availability" offers an opportunity but doesn't indicate need or change.

L2, Need, defines a customer's desire that can be satisfied or exceeded by your services. Be aware that customers typically have a wide range of implied, stated, or unstated needs. These needs can be classified into two broad categories: increasing or improving a good situation and decreasing or minimizing a bad situation. However, note the distinction: Needs differ from change because they lack the commitment to take any action. For example, a customer might say, "We have been thinking about talking to a vendor to improve product availability because we have been receiving complaints from customers." This statement indicates a need to improve the situation, not a desire to change vendors. After all, the customer may believe that the situation can be rectified with the current vendor.

The most critical level of interest is L3, Recognition for Change. I define this as the process of uncovering the customer's actual problem, moving beyond a need for change to the absolute understanding of the customer's need for continuing actions. Uncovering the need for change motivates the customer to take action and to make a commitment to correct the situation. And it's up to you to move the customer off the dime. For example, the customer may say something like, "We've been thinking about talking to a vendor to improve product availability because we've been receiving complaints from customers, and if we don't correct the problem, we'll lose money and clients." It's up to you to move the customer from that recognition to a follow-through on change.

Not All Needs Are Fulfilled

We all have needs for something, but we don't always recognize the need to change and make the commitment to alter the situation. For example, a few years ago my wife kept bugging me that we needed to get a new refrigerator. My response was usually, "We will." I happened to like our old one. I thought it nicely fit in with our kitchen. One day she pointed out an appliance ad to me with refrigerators on sale. There was one in particular she liked, and the price seemed reasonable. There was our opportunity. Would you believe that within a few days the milk started going sour and something smelled funny in the meat bin whenever I opened the door? I began to see a need for a new refrigerator. The next day I grabbed the milk carton and to my horror poured out milk chunks on my morning cereal. The ice cream was melting on the floor, and I had to toss out the green lunch meat. What do you think I did? Like any self-respecting husband, I yelled, "Annette, I need you. We need a new refrigerator." There was my recognition of the need for change, so we went out that afternoon to the appliance sale and bought a new refrigerator.

That was a change we were able to fulfill. My unrequited dream for a 1968 Shelby Convertible Mustang remains a wish because, if for no other reason, I can't fit two car seats in the back and another child plus my wife in the front. Besides, that car costs a small fortune, so that's one need that can't be fulfilled, no matter how much I think I need it.

All salespeople have been trained to uncover a customer's needs, but, as my Shelby story illustrates, more often than not the customer doesn't end up buying to fulfill her needs. Of course, this presents yet another challenge for CSRs, who have been taught that when a customer has a problem and a need, their job is to meet it. You can still do that while you cross the bridge to your proactive role, but you are simply solving the customer's needs in a different manner and using a new set of tools. The customer's needs are different now, but so are the techniques to solve them.

As we've been discussing, the concepts of L1, L2, and L3 (creating new opportunities, identifying needs, mobilizing the need to change) will get your customer moving in the right direction, but to get to closure, you really need to move her to L3. Remember, L1 lacks a clear statement or desire to correct the situation at hand, and L2 lacks a commitment to take action. Only L3 truly uncovers the customer's need for change and motivates the customer to take action and make a commitment to correct the situation. What tool do I recommend to guide you through this particular process? I call it funneling. In Chapter 7 I'll explain how this technique can help you mix together the information you've gathered about your customer, which will serve as the basis for creating the right buying atmosphere. Now, we don't use a funnel to make glop, but I guarantee the process will help make your customer hungry for your product or service.

7

"I Thought a Funnel Was for Cooking"

Funneling as a Vehicle for Change

At this point, I can't help wondering whether you're beginning to sound like my kids sitting in the backseat during almost any length car ride—fifteen minutes or fifteen hours: "Are we there yet?" So I'll tell you what I usually tell them. "No, we're not there yet, but it's not much longer, so just sit back and enjoy the ride." Besides, the tactics I discuss in this chapter, if used correctly, can actually shorten the ride and put you in the driver's seat.

As we discussed in Chapter 6, we are unable to move forward until we secure our customer's agreement to change his habits. Remember that story I told you about our broken refrigerator? When it was just acting up, our family had a need, but when it really broke down and the milk got sour and chunky, I went quickly from having a need to agreeing to change. When your customer recognizes her own willingness to take a closer look at your company's services and products, and that agreement to change is accomplished through continuing questioning, you're really on your way. But for insurance, you also need to include countering questions, along with the listening funnel, the focus of this chapter. Couple this with the skills you learned in the "half" of the quarter-half-quarter model and you'll be able to distinguish yourself from the competition because you'll have gained a better understanding of the customer's situation. By adding the funneling process, you can cement the relationship and create an atmosphere of trust, agreement, and complete disclosure. Remember, as a proactive CSR, the three elements you're selling now are a relationship, the required need for change, and, eventually, a solution—but still not your product or service.

Generally, people don't make a move to fix or change something until they recognize the implications of a lack of action. For example, you might put up with that annoying dripping ceiling for months and not bother to call a roofer until you realize the leak has rotted out the wooden supports and much of your plaster ceiling. Then you desperately call a contractor and demand he come over as soon as possible. When you get the bill, and your spouse is sputtering over your shoulder, you finally recognize the implications (as well as the consequences) of your inaction.

What Is Funneling?

I define funneling as linking a series of questions (probing, MLPQ, and countering) that focus on the topic under discussion. The intention is to engage a customer in an in-depth dialogue to reveal information and generate a willingness to change. We're still in the "half" part of the quarter-half-quarter model, but the next few elements I'll address are intended to sweeten your approach and offer some additional tools to your overall selling approach.

The Components of a Funnel

Now, let's look at the components of a funnel (Figure 7-1). First of all, it does, indeed, resemble a typical kitchen funnel, but it lacks a handle (no need to hold onto it), and it's flat and sealed on the bottom. Although, unlike a real funnel, it doesn't contain any holes to let liquid seep out, it does serve as a container to carry and mix components of consultative selling. Also, you can open or close the funnel—open it with questions, close it when

Figure 7-1.   Components of a funnel.

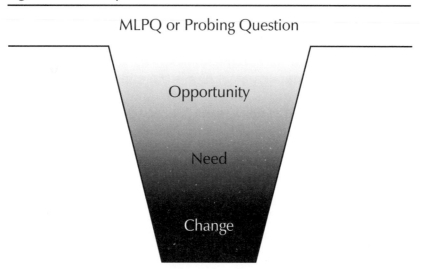

MLPQ or Probing Question

Opportunity

Need

Change

you receive a customer response to your final area of interest. At the top of the funnel, you add MLPQs and probing questions. Those gradually mix to produce opportunity, need, and change. Remember, this is another device for you to use to reach your goal of convincing your customer to acknowledge the need for change. Once again, questioning techniques play a vital role in applying the funnel properly and effectively, as do listening and information-gathering skills. The objective is ultimately to convince the customer to change his attitudes, habits, and so on. That's why this technique can be so critical to the process of moving on to the presentation.

The Funneling Process

Let's look at the primary funneling process, composed of five steps (Figure 7-2). After each step, assume there's a customer response:

1. Ask a multilayered or dialogue-probing question.
2. Listen and identify the initial words that start the customer's sentence. Ask a question to get the person to reveal more information surrounding her choice of words (e.g., "thinking about," "considering," "looking at").

Figure 7-2. The funnel formula.

Step 1	Ask a probing question.
Step 2	Monitor the customer's initial response.
Step 3	Trace the history of the response.
Step 4	Expand the list of needed items, and explore the response.
Step 5	Move the customer to an agreement to change.

3. Trace the "history" of the person's response. Explore the past events that led to her current situation or response.
4. Identify and expand the "list" of needed items or problem areas she mentioned, recognize what was said, explore what wasn't said. Respond with: "You mention X and Y; tell me the other areas you evaluated prior to selecting these two."
5. Ask the customer what is happening in all of the areas identified. To close the funnel, ask your customer: "If all things remain the same, what will be the effect on your department, company, or project?"

Now that you know the process, what are the consultative selling elements it is addressing? At the top are MLPQs and probing questions, which, moving down the funnel, generate opportunity, need, and change. Some additional rules for using the funnel include:

1. The MLPQ and probing questions should be based on the customer's issues (objective).
2. Don't change the subject of the conversation in the funnel.
3. Don't offer your own opinion.
4. Apply three to four funnels, each addressing a separate issue (objective) of the customer in the "half" section of the quarter-half-quarter model.

How do you know when you've reached the bottom of your funnel? Obviously, when the prospect has acknowledged the need for change, and you have overcome any objections he may have raised. (We'll look at objections more closely in Chapter 10.) At this level, you summarize the customer's needs. "As I understand it, Mr. Roberts, you need some new computer software that can manage your distribution system, which has been reshuffled, but you don't want to toss away your old system, which serves as the lifeline of your company." And you hear his acknowledgment for a need to change. "Yes, we certainly need some expertise to help us reconfigure what we have so that we can more accurately manage our distribution channels." His response indicates trust, agreement, and complete disclosure. You're almost there.

Persuading a customer to acknowledge the need for change also requires you to listen closely, a necessary element in almost every technique and situation. When we get to the "how to overcome objections" section, you'll see how listening plays an integral role there, too.

The Funnel Is Really an Interview

When you're funneling, think of yourself as actually interviewing the customer. The conversational tone of MLPQs that we discussed in Chapter 6 works well in this context. As anyone who has to interview people on a regular basis can tell you—reporters, for example—asking questions, listening for the answers, and paying attention to the circumstances is really an art that reporters must learn to execute well. That old reporter friend of mine that I mentioned earlier is convinced that nonverbal cues such as leaning forward, shaking of the head, voice inflections, facial expressions, and body movement also play a role in the way a person communicates. In the course of an interview, the subject may ramble on, his voice may go up or down in response to a particularly uncomfortable question, or he may even yell.

Reporters interview people over the telephone as well as in person, so they must learn how to sense many of the same cues that CSRs need to learn about. CSRs are rarely in adversarial settings with customers, but they should still pay attention to:

- The fabric and feel of the talk
- How they respond to a given answer
- Keeping control of the direction of the conversation
- Timing (knowing when to be silent, when to say something, and when to be more aggressive or passive)
- Impact of statements
- Recognizing emotion
- Maintaining a sense of friendliness

By analyzing how customers respond during the conversation, you learn more about them and their situations than they convey on the surface and by their words. You can then use this information to support your questions and help you move down the funnel until you hit the objective of this technique—persuading the customer to acknowledge the need for change—with the basic premise being, "We certainly need a product that can help us improve that situation."

Using the Funnel

You can close the funnel with a question designed to confirm that the customer has, indeed, come to the conclusion that he has to make a change. What you're looking to say is something like, "Based upon our discussion, are you willing to take the necessary steps to change?" That's it, folks. But, to be frank, you're not quite ready for that yet. Let me first give you some additional hints and illustrations to strengthen your understanding of funneling.

An important initial point to remember is that you will be using more than one funnel, because most likely you will need to discuss at least four to five issues with your customers. When you complete one funnel, you simply move on to the next, preferably by using a conversational bridge (Figure 7-3) of some kind. "You know, I find that safety issue really interesting. Do you have similar concerns with other work issues? If that's the

Figure 7-3.   Using a conversational bridge to move from one issue to another.

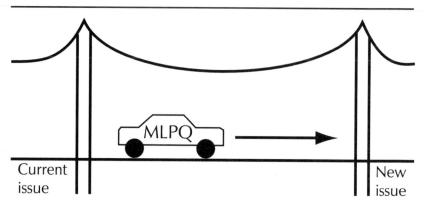

case, please tell me about your experience with one of those issues compared with the safety problems."

Completing the funneling process requires the use of all five steps. Because the funnel is designed to convince the customer to recognize a need for change, you move through the funnel by executing all the steps while refraining from presenting a solution until you get that change commitment. This can be difficult, and it requires discipline on your part, but if in your enthusiasm you do skip one of the steps, don't be surprised if you find you need to return to that step or even start all over again.

Let's look at the five major steps again, but this time in more detail.

Step 1

Ask the dialogue or MLPQ question.

Step 2

Identify important words (e.g., we, I, thinking about, looking at, considering, asked, mandated, required, hope to, should, moving toward), and ask the customer to expand on them.

Step 3

Recognize that almost any response has a "history." Ask a question that goes back to the past. Explore the course of events that led to the customer's current position, condition, and decision to deal with the issue now (e.g., "Considering that most companies in your industry are now required to adhere to the newest environmental regulations, how do these regs compare with how you dealt with these issues under the old rules?").

Step 4

Expand the list of problem areas by using the following question: "You mentioned A and B. Tell me about the other areas you considered prior to selecting these two."

Step 5

To end the funnel, ask, "If everything remains the same, what will be the impact on your. . . ."

Let's assume you've gotten your commitment to change from your customer. I can almost hear the trumpets sounding. Now your task is to summarize the key points. Ask if there are any additional areas to review. Specifically, ask, "Do you want to take steps to correct and resolve this situation?"

Even if you, as a CSR, don't receive a yes answer, all is not lost. It probably means the customer doesn't see a need for change. Don't blame yourself. Maybe he wasn't listening closely, or maybe the issue didn't strike a serious enough chord with him. In any case, begin another funnel with another issue (remember, you should have at least three or four), and repeat the five-step process.

During the course of the funneling step explanations, I referred to a couple of concepts that are pretty obvious but that need additional descriptions so that you can see how they fit into the funneling process. The first is a questioning technique known as "countering." A countering question requires a lot of listening on your part. Basically, it's a follow-up question that depends on repeating one word or phrase or idea that the customer mentioned in his previous response. It helps you identify and explore the key words in your customer's response to your previous question. The key words either begin or end the final sentence phrase. Countering involves looking for information that you can use to get your customer to commit to change, but it tends to be more subtle than MLPQ or dialogue questions.

Some Funneling Exercises

You must follow the five steps of the funneling process when you ask your countering question so that you have five more pieces of information to add to the funnel. Let's try a couple of exercises and see how you do. Go back and review the five major steps of funneling. Keep your finger on that page, because you'll need to refer to it for the following exercises.

Here is the customer response for which we will be choosing the best countering question for Steps 2 and 3 of the funneling process:

Customer Response: "We're trying to put a new system in place in the next three months, even though we're short-staffed."

1. Select the best option Step 2 counterquestion that identifies and explores the key words that begin the customer response.

    a. What's happening? Is there something hampering your efforts?
    b. Balancing a short staff while attempting to move forward can be a challenge. Can you describe for me how it's going?
    c. It sounds like this has been a demanding task. Who has been involved in this project?
    d. What type of staff do you have? Why is a three-month period so critical?

In this exercise, the best choice is "c" because it's a way of identifying who the decision makers are by responding to the "We" in the customer's statement.

Let's try the next one.
2. Select the best option for Step 3, in which you trace the history of the customer's response.

    a. Tell me about the course of events that led to the need for a new system.
    b. Selecting the right system is important. What do you want it to do?
    c. Do you believe you will make the deadline?
    d. If we could provide you with staffing to assist in the installation and training, would this be of interest to you?

This time the correct answer is "a," because Step 3 relates to the "history" of the company or a time element, and so does the question. I might also point out that the last choice, "d," is to be avoided at all costs at this point of the sales process, for a couple of reasons: It offers a solution to the problem, but you're not there yet, and it talks about your own company's skills, which is a no-no in the "half" section of the quarter-half-quarter model.

Now let's try working with another version of the customer's response and see how you do with that:

Customer Response: "We're trying to put a new system in place in the next three months because of our concern for accuracy and the need to lower labor costs."

3. Select the best option for a Step 4 counterquestion.

    a. Accuracy and labor are issues that need to be addressed. What is happening with your present system that you feel a need to replace your existing equipment?
    b. How is your current system performing in these areas?
    c. You mentioned accuracy and lower labor costs. Tell me the other areas you evaluated prior to identifying these two.
    d. How much do you want to lower costs? How would you rate your current quality standards?

The answer for this Step 4 response is "c" because it contains the key word, "prior," and expands the list of problem areas.

Let's take a break from the countering exercises and listen to a story that I happen to especially like, not only because it involves my daughter but because it illustrates moving from recognizing a need and moving to a commitment for change. About a year ago my wife began talking about how our five-year-old should have a computer because, after all, in these days of technology and with kids as young as two "surfing the Net," our daughter was probably already behind her schoolmates. I reluctantly agreed that we should start looking around at computers.

Initially, when I put on my sales training hat, I realized that my agreement to look at computers represented an action step. We finally narrowed our choice to two computers. And then my daughter turned six years old, and she still didn't have a computer. Why? Because we acknowledged the need for a computer for my daughter, but we didn't yet see a reason for a commitment to change. And until that need intensified and we understood the consequences of our inaction, our daughter still wouldn't have a computer.

Well, guess what. That was our attitude until recently, a year after we first talked about getting a computer. Once again my wife said we needed to get a computer for our now six-year-old daughter (I guess she had gotten even further behind those overachieving two-year-olds). I responded, "You're right." Meanwhile, we had decided that my wife was going to get involved in my company, setting up some new financial systems. With an infant, it was tough for her to come to the office on any kind of regular schedule, so we decided that it made sense to get a computer at home that she could connect to our office system and use at home when she couldn't get to the office. What a great idea, and yes, we recently bought a computer. And, yes, my daughter uses it, too.

What does this story tell us? Not only did we recognize the need; we finally made the commitment to change. Mind you, we felt a dual need—to have my wife work out of home and to enable my daughter to practice her ABC's on the computer.

How can you relate to this story? You know that every customer has a list of needs, some longer than others, and as varied as snowflakes, depending on the topic. Your job, as an inside sales CSR, is not only to identify the needs of your customers and determine how they relate to your product line but also to look at your own profession. With these new challenges, you are forced to reexamine your own need to succeed. As a traditional

CSR, you fulfilled your customer's need as well as your own by satisfying the customer's request. Now you're moving up to a new kind of self-need satisfaction quotient.

Let's imagine for a minute that you're a salesperson in an upscale men's clothing store. A customer is browsing around the $500 suits and then begins picking up the $75 ties and holding them in front of a mirror. As a commissioned salesperson, you'd love to sell him a suit and a tie, but you also know that once someone buys the more expensive item, it's no big deal to buy the less expensive item also. So if you can sell the man the $500 suit, it's likely you'll also be able to sell him that $75 tie to go with the suit. Yet, if he comes in and looks only at the ties, that $75 is going to represent a much bigger decision on his part, and he's less likely to buy the tie, let alone a $500 suit.

It's like the McDonald's "Supersize" promotion. When you order a meal and the order taker asks you if you want to "Supersize" it, it will cost you an extra thirty-nine cents, in addition to the $3 or $4 you're already spending on your meal. Once you've made the commitment to buy the more expensive item, it's much easier to make the decision to spend an additional lesser amount. In fact, many times you don't even give it much thought.

It's the same thing with a new car. I must say, I really admire how the automakers have mastered this technique. If you're buying a $15,000 car that comes without floor mats or a stereo, are you really going to balk at the salesperson's suggestion that you spend an additional $150 for the stereo system? Of course not, even though you could walk into any electronics store and buy a similar system for less, and you certainly won't end up financing $150 over a three- to four-year period.

Here's the problem. As traditional CSRs, you've been busy selling the ties and fries, the cheaper items; for the most part, you haven't been selling the big-ticket items. CSRs are certainly not used to saying to their customers, "For another $100 I can sell you fries or ties." In other words, CSRs have focused on selling the accessories and extra warranties while someone else sold the expensive item that went with them. In the context of this book, the outside sales force has been used to selling the suits. But now, CSRs can sell the sports coats and maybe some extra cheese and bacon on their burgers. Using the clothing metaphor, to do this successfully, you need to see that the person sees a need for adding to his wardrobe and a change of clothes. At the beginning of your transition, perhaps you were selling the cuff links that went with the suit, and have since moved up to selling the ties. But now it's time to make the transition once again to selling the bigger ticket item. And that's what this funneling process is all about. It builds your skills so that you're capable of selling that expensive item—and maybe more than one.

Before we leave this subject, I'd like to give you a more complete funneling flow chart that you can refer to during your next challenging sales call.

Funneling Flow Chart

Question 1   Ask a series of informational open/ closed probe questions to gather initial information.

Customer Response:

Question 2   "Describe for me _____, and how does it compare to _____."
(Step 1 counter—ask dialogue-probing question)

Customer Response:

Question 3   "It sounds like you have given this some thought. Who has been involved in this process, and how is it going?"
(Step 2 counter—identifying the key decision makers)

Customer Response:

Question 4   "You mentioned _____. Tell me about the course of events that led you to respond in that way."
(Step 3 counter—tracing the history)

Customer Response:

Question 5   "You know, I read an article the other day about _____ in *The Wall Street Journal.* Did you happen to see the story?"

Customer Response: "Yes, I did," or "No, I didn't."

CSR: "What the article went on to say was that many departments are concerned with _____. As a matter of fact, it seems that others in the same marketplace who were interviewed agree with this position. Describe for me your experience in this area. How does it compare with what the article suggests?"

Customer Response:

Question 6   "During our conversation, we have talked about several areas, X and Y. What were some of the other areas you evaluated prior to identifying these two?" (Step 4 counter—expanding the list)

Customer Response:

Question 7   "Tell me about the history that prompted you to identify those/that issue." (repeat of Step 3 counter)

Customer Response:

Question 8   "Tell me more. What is happening in these areas?"

Customer Response:

Question 9   "We've talked a lot about several issues that are concerning you. What would be the impact on your department if everything remained the same?" (Step 5 counter—seeking change)

Summary of Issues—Closing the Funnel

Question 10 "Are there any other issues we need to talk about?"

Customer Response:

Question 11 "On the basis of our discussion, are you willing to take steps to correct the condition?"

I hope this flow chart has clarified any questions you may have had about how funneling works and how you can use it effectively. Just to check, I have a couple of brief exercises to run past you. (I hope you don't think I'm getting carried away with tests and exercises, but I believe they help you identify your own strengths and weaknesses.) For these exercises, you should refer to the three counterquestion exercises we did earlier, because those multiple-answer choices apply to these, too.

1. Write a Step 2 counterquestion that explores and identifies the key words that start the sentence.
   Customer response to MLPQ: "We have been looking at a new system that offers faster access." (Focus on key words at the beginning of the response and ask for further clarification or information about what they said.)

_____

_____

_____

The correct answer is "c" from the first countering exercise ("It sounds like this has been a demanding task. Who has been involved in this project?").

2. Write a Step 3 counterquestion that explores and identifies the history or course of events that led to the customer's current position or comments.

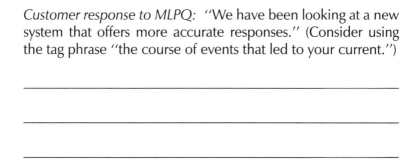

Customer response to MLPQ: "We have been looking at a new system that offers more accurate responses." (Consider using the tag phrase "the course of events that led to your current.")

The correct answer is "a" from the second countering exercise ("Tell me about the course of events that led to the need for a new system").

OK. No more exercises for a while. Let's relax a bit and talk about politics—well, not really. When former Vice President Dan Quayle published his book, *The American Family*, he made the rounds of the morning talk shows promoting the book. One morning Katie Couric on the *Today* show interviewed Mr. Quayle about the book and asked him what criteria he had used to assess whether a family was functioning successfully. He explained that he had researched the book on families by talking to five functional families from around the country with diverse backgrounds and ethnicity. Despite their problems, he considered these five families successful because they had maintained their middle-class values without any help from the government.

My immediate response was, "Well, fancy that." Mr. Quayle managed to write a book that purported to investigate middle-class values by interviewing only five selected families. We know well that dysfunctional families with all sorts of problems and characteristics (e.g., drug and alcohol abuse) exist all around us and also possess these so-called middle-class values. Yet, Mr. Quayle chose to talk to only five families that supported his own theories. Real authentic, huh? That's probably why the book didn't sell so well.

It doesn't matter whether or not I supported Mr. Quayle. I'm looking at his methodology. From our research and questioning experience, we know that the list of characteristics of functional families is much more inclusive, and it was incumbent on him to reveal all the traits that list contained, instead of focusing on just a few characteristics. The point here is, when you are funneling, don't let the customer get away without giving you a complete list of factors that affect his business. If you get the customer to expand the list, you are able to build on your selling process by using the additional information and eventually wangle a commitment to change.

We're ready to move on to Chapter 8, where we'll examine the almighty decision makers, who they are and how we can get to them. They're the ones who can make or break our deals. So, go ahead, take a break, but don't stay away for long. I think you'll like this next one.

8

"Can I Speak With What's-His-or-Her-Name, Please?"

Determining the Decision Makers and Sales Cycle Techniques

Remember the last time you got angry with a sales clerk, a company store representative, or another service employee, such as an insurance rep? Maybe the company had made an error on your billing, wouldn't honor your insurance claim, or sold you an item that was damaged and wouldn't take it back. Did you angrily ask the name of the clerk's supervisor and ask to talk to her? Maybe you ended up moving even further up the company ladder until you received some kind of satisfaction for your complaint. And at each step, you got the executive's name. You might even have ended up with the president's name and address. (Word to the wise—I have a friend who uses that technique often because she finds it tends to move things along pretty rapidly.)

Now, with my tongue firmly in my cheek, I'm sure nothing like that has ever happened to any CSR reading this book. I also realize that some customers can be totally unreasonable, and sometimes there's not a darn thing anyone can do about it. But that's not the kind of situation I want to talk about here.

In my example, you need to find a decision maker who can solve your problem for you. You're probably steaming, so it's not too difficult to ask for the clerk's supervisor. In this chapter, however, I'm going to talk about the need to find out who the customer-company decision maker is, but for an entirely different reason. You won't be a bit angry, just seeking the person who has the authority to make the commitment to change. In the illustration, you want your problem solved. In advanced consultation selling, you need the customer to agree to change her buying habits and make a commitment to take action.

Many times your company contact—the person who calls you frequently and with whom you feel comfortable talking—is not the person who can make the final decision. I admit that it's probably easier to simply ask for the supervisor than, in an enthusiastic but mild manner, to ask your contact whom you need to speak with to get a decision. That's why I'm going to give you guiding points and illustrations to help you move through this step by applying some of the techniques we've already discussed. This will also help you better understand how some of the strategies can be interchangeable and added to the half-quarter-half equation when you need them so that you can finally move into your solution-presentation mode.

Reading the Signals

As we've already discussed, CSRs have already established some kind of relationship with their customers, although it's a business relationship in which they call for a reason, and you make sure they're satisfied. But when you begin asking questions—recital, dialogue-probing, MLPQs—this adds something new to the relationship. Due to your preparation, you know what you're going to say, but you don't really know how the customer will respond. So you have to be especially tuned in to listen to the response and make sure you hear what's really said, not what you wanted to hear. Consider this illustration that my men readers may be able to relate to.

Think way back to your early dating experiences. This may be painful, but humor me for just a minute. Here's the scene.

You've finally worked up the nerve to talk with the girl you've admired from afar. After stammering and stuttering, you finally ask her out on a date to see a movie on the upcoming Friday. She's on her way to class, so she responds with, "Why don't you give me a call? We'll talk about it then." You're walking on Cloud Nine while you mentally run through what you'll say to her and how she'll be enchanted with your sense of humor and lively personality. Then you work up the nerve to call her, and she says, "I'm sorry, but I'm busy on Friday. Maybe some other time." You feel deflated and totally despondent. After all, she had expressed interest when she suggested you call. But had she really accepted your invitation to go to a movie with you? No, and you, in your enthusiasm to take her out on a date, overlooked what she really said. She never accepted the offer but instead gave you a signal that you misinterpreted.

You can now put that agonizing experience behind you as long as you understand the point of that story. We've already discussed how to categorize the interest of your customers so that you don't jump ahead of the game, make unrealistic assumptions, and try to move forward in the selling cycle or even close the sale before your contact is ready. Remember the three levels of interest: negative, noncommittal, and positive. A negative response to your questions indicates disinterest, skepticism, and/or resistance. By now, you can instinctively feel when you're getting a negative response, such as "You tell a convincing story." The customer doesn't seem really interested. The noncommittal response is the most common. In this case the customer indicates an impartial attitude toward your ideas or solutions. She doesn't give you any indication of her actual intent but may say things like "Your people really seem to understand our problem." Sure, that's a nice comment, like "call me and we'll talk," but it doesn't really tell you that she intends to buy your product or service. The most constructive response, which is categorized as positive, is a comment that is supportive, encouraging, or optimistic and that actually gives signs of intent to act. That can be a response like "I like the idea. I'll talk to the committee about it" or "We could have used this last year. This will work well with our new operation." Remember, what you're listening for is an indication of action.

Qualifying the Customer's Response

It's not always easy to qualify the customer's responses. One thing to watch for is what I call "futuring." In your eagerness to make the sale, you inaccurately interpret a customer's comments as buying signals, when he's actually putting you off: "I like your proposal. Let me call you about it." That's futuring. He's really putting you off, if you let him. To get around that, I try to create the future in the present by qualifying the customer's statements so that I can truly understand the intent and meaning of his statements. With the previous example, you might respond, "I know you're busy. When should I expect a phone call from you? Or, maybe I'll just call you on Friday to see what you think." With this comment, you are forcing a specific action and stopping him from "futuring" you.

Another technique that helps overcome futuring is what I call a "transparent qualifier." When you're trying to overcome futuring, you can gain useful information from the client about what specific conversations or activities might occur in the future. For example, you might ask a client who has requested information from you when he plans to be done reviewing it or when he plans to schedule a meeting with the decision makers to present the information to them. This not only furthers the conversation but also helps you learn about your customer's positive or negative feelings regarding your product or service. In addition, it can help you determine your customer's actual interest level.

Here's another example. Following a business meeting with a potential client on a Wednesday, a friend of mine who's a consultant—I'll call her Jane—was asked to prepare an extensive proposal for a major project for the client by Friday. She requested some background materials to aid her efforts, so an assistant was sent scurrying around to find the materials. When she returned empty-handed, the company president said they would find what she needed that afternoon. Jane asked that, because the time frame was so tight, they send the material by their messenger service; otherwise, she told them, she couldn't possibly meet their deadline. The potential client's office was in the city; Jane's office was in a nearby suburb. After a brief hesitation, the company president said that maybe they really didn't need the proposal until the next partners meeting and suggested she write the proposal once she received his company materials. P.S. This company never did hire a consultant for its all-important project.

What do you think happened here? In situations like Jane's, as well as in sales, it's quite common for potential clients to ask the salesperson or consultant for information—or even for a proposal—without having given a serious indication that they really intend to buy. Even though Jane had spent an hour meeting with the company president and some of his associates, she still didn't know his interest level; in short, he was futuring her. To jar an action out of him, and move the future to the present, she asked him to messenger the materials to her at his expense. This response forced him to take an action and let her know how serious he really was about her services. Obviously, he wasn't all that serious, after all. Fortunately, because Jane had been through these kinds of antics before, she had made sure to schedule this meeting on the same afternoon that she had scheduled other client meetings, so the hour with the supposed new client was not a great waste of her time.

It's unlikely you will ever encounter a situation like this as an inside sales representative. However, a similar situation could occur over the telephone, with a customer indicating an interest by asking for information from you. The trick, obviously, is to accurately gauge your customer's interest by recognizing some of the most common "put-off" techniques that customers use and creating responses that can help you accurately identify those responses. By doing this you can move the customer to your side of the playing field. In other words, these techniques can help you achieve account penetration (uncovering more opportunities and decision makers), which can ultimately help you figure out your critical path or how you're going to proceed. Remember, you want to be in control, not the customer.

Sales managers need to remember that, by assessing customer interest, CSRs will be qualifying customers' responses while moving toward a sales solution. And their real advantage is knowing the customer. After all, ultimately a CSR's goal is to cross-sell another product. For example, if you're a computer software company that also sells hardware, you may have a CSR who's been dealing with a customer for six months—and the customer is in the process of revamping its management information systems. What luck!

But in order to capitalize on this relationship, it's important for the CSR to recognize who this regular contact person is and what his responsibilities may be. As I pointed out earlier, the person calling your CSR to place an order, ask a question, or get additional information may not be the person with the authority to make a buying decision. In fact, he probably isn't, because he doesn't control spending. Frequently, the contact is a member of the purchasing department, putting through orders received from other departments. The salesperson's job, or the CSR's job, is to find out who does make the buying decisions.

Maintaining F.A.C.E.

I've created an acronym to make it easier for you to locate people with power at your customer's company. Just remember the word "face." F is for the financial person, A is for the applier, C is for the champion, and E is for the evaluator. This is how F.A.C.E. works (Figure 8-1).

During the course of the conversation, the CSR questions the contact person to identify the people who make up the F.A.C.E. F may stand for the financial person, but it doesn't necessarily have to be the top finance official or even the controller; it can be someone who approves spending at the company. A stands for appliers, the people who would come in daily contact

Figure 8-1.   Identifying the decision makers.

F	inancial officer
A	pplier
C	hampion
E	valuator

with your company's new product or service. To find out who these people are, try using a multilayered question: "Tell me, who is a co-worker who uses our products regularly? Is that person in the sales department?" *C* stands for "champion"; I'll get back to this in a minute. *E* stands for evaluator, the person who evaluates the performance of your product and determines whether you're one of the players the company will consider.

Now let's return to *C*, for champion. It's critical to have a champion for your cause. If your CSR does have an enduring—say, six-month—relationship with a customer, we hope this person is a buddy by now. The champion—we'll call her Helen—can refer you to the person who makes new product decisions. Say the evaluator is a team; Helen could refer you to the one person who can act on your request. Maybe there are 400 appliers. Obviously you can't get to all of them, but Helen could certainly identify the manager for you and make an introduction on your behalf. She can also support your efforts by helping you understand the pulse of the company. In short, she wants to see you win, because then she wins, too, by looking good to her superiors.

You can see that the people you identify by using F.A.C.E. represent four different roles in the company. Ideally, the financial person and your champion are the same person. Usually it's just one person, but sometimes it can be a committee. This is true for evaluators and appliers as well. Obviously, you can't get to all of them, but you should be able to reach at least a supervisor or manager. And your champion is the means to that end. How might you do that? For example, after several months of talking with Helen, a purchasing agent with the Widget Company, you say to her, "Helen, we've known each other for a long time, and you've been a great customer. I enjoy our conversations, and I appreciated your advice on dealing with my teenage daughter. But now I could use your help in a different way. I'm trying to get in touch with regular, quality customers for a new product we're selling, but I need to know who the right person is to talk to about this at your company. Could you help me out?"

No doubt, a champion like Helen will want to help you and even act as a coach, giving you tips such as how to deal with Mr.

Smith or whomever. She can even give you a reference and prop you up as someone who knows his stuff. The ultimate champion might order 100 pieces from you when she needs only fifty. Bless Helen.

And bless my contact at a major national corporation. At this particular company, the CSRs are now known as strategic sales representatives and are part of its sales team. The CSRs help to build customer relationships, especially when they use the advanced consultative selling techniques we've been discussing. The views of the company's strategic services manager take this CSR approach a step further. F.A.C.E. is a favorite technique of hers because it gives her the opportunity to establish a multilevel penetration through her CSRs as well as the sales reps. Listen.

"It offers the chance to build more relationships with others at the company," she says. Then she relates that point to the concept of turning CSRs into an inside sales operation. "For example, the sales rep might be working with the chief financial officer while the CSR is working with accounts receivable or the MIS operation. The roles are becoming interchangeable. Think about your target. When you have a target it gives you more flexibility to meet that target because the CSR is not viewed as a traditional salesperson, so the customer is much more receptive."

Thank you for those observations. I took another gulp of coffee after she told me her views, especially her perception regarding customers' reaction to CSRs compared to the sales reps. It's a refreshing approach to them. Now let's put on an even happier face. Let's assume Helen has done her job well and identified the key players for you. What do you do next? You create what I call a critical path of account penetration, or your sales cycle. This is much more than just arbitrarily plotting out how you plan to succeed.

Using the Quarter-Half-Quarter Model to Plan Your Sales Cycle

Remember the quarter-half-quarter model? It serves as the central component of this process, so you need to use it as your visual cue to help map out your sales cycle. Up to now, we've really focused on the "half" part as a means of building a relationship with your customer by asking the right kinds of questions and convincing him to make a commitment to change. Now we're going to look at how to use the entire model to help you design your sales plan.

Ultimately you want to map out when you should present your solution, because if you present it too soon, you may end up shooting yourself in the foot, or, to use my favorite football metaphors, you may rush to the thirty-yard line when the play calls for you to be at the forty-yard line.

With that in mind, here come some more steps again—but these are really common sense, and my intent here is to build your awareness of this approach so that it will become a natural part of the CSR sales process. Your sales cycle has a beginning, a middle, and an end. For example, the phone call you receive from the credit card company or bank encouraging you to get another credit card is a one-cycle sale, as are makeup demonstrations and other in-home kinds of sales. The salesperson does everything in one step. Then there are the three- and five-step cycles. With a three-step cycle, the first step may be to build a relationship; the second step to give a proposal/solution; and the third step, to close. The next most common sales cycle is the five-step cycle: step one builds the relationship, step two creates a relationship with other decision makers, step three offers your proposal/solutions, step four is a demonstration or trial of service, and step five is the close. In every one of these steps, you have minimum, primary, and secondary actions (see Figure 8-2):

Minimum	The least you want to accomplish during the call or conversation. If you are executing Step 2 in your cycle (presenting a proposal), your minimum action is to explain the proposal.
Primary	Acceptance to move to the next step in the cycle. If you have executed Step 2 in your cycle, your primary objective is to obtain agreement to proceed to Step 3: close.

Figure 8-2.   Plotting minimum, primary, and secondary actions.

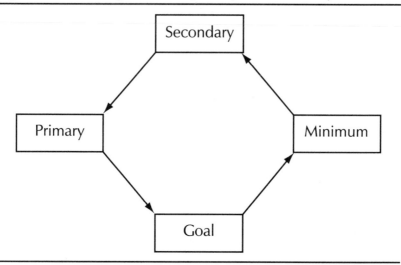

Secondary   This is known as Plan "B." If you can't reach
                 agreement to your call's primary objective,
                 the next best action would be a secondary
                 agreement indicating their interest to pro-
                 ceed (i.e.: willingness to change or seeing
                 your product/service as a solution).

The trick is to take the time to determine your cycle and identify
your actions to measure the progression of the relationship process. This isn't a one-time analysis, either.

Minimum, Primary, and Secondary Actions

Every step of the way, it's incumbent on you to determine the
minimum primary and secondary actions that will allow you to
move on to the next step. For example, in creating the initial
relationship, the minimum action may simply be to come back
to see the customer or to arrange to talk to him again on the
phone; a secondary action might be to determine the key players; a primary action might be to identify an area for continuing
discovery (or for seeking additional information). Under "continued discovery" as a second step, your minimum action could

be to receive additional information on specialized areas; your secondary action could be meeting and initiating relationships with key players; and your primary action could be the creation of a willingness to change on the client's part and an appointment to conduct an on-site visit.

Did those examples help explain how to map out your minimum, secondary, and primary moves for each step? Good. What's probably most important to remember while figuring out your sales cycle is that once you determine what your cycle will be, that cycle never changes, but how you get there and how long it takes you to get through each step will.

To perhaps help clarify this concept a bit more for you, imagine a baseball diamond, with first base, second, third, and home. You always have to go from first base to second base to third base before scoring a run. Maybe the first time at bat your hit lands you at first base—the first step in the cycle, if you will. The next hitter gets a single. But you have to run to second base before you can run to third base (the third step in the cycle). That hit allowed you to move quickly from first base to third, but you still had to make sure you touched second base, too.

Now you're at third base, your best hitter is up to bat, there are two outs, and you're behind by one run. A bunt by the batter lets you score. That's a four-step cycle, which is not common in sales but works for our illustration. Maybe you hit a home run when you're up to bat. That's one step, but you still have to go around the field and touch all the bases. Now, let's say you're on second base, and you try to steal third. You get halfway there, realize you're going to get thrown out, and run back to second. How does this fit into your sales cycle? Sometimes you think you've completed a step—say, a client's commitment to buy— but early on in the next step it becomes increasingly apparent that you really don't have that commitment after all. So you have to repeat step two, or, in our baseball analogy, return to second base.

With each of these steps, you've got your minimum, primary, and secondary actions already determined, but the cycle never changes. For example, let's say your third step is to present your proposal and solution (you're in the last quarter of the model). Your minimum action is to accomplish explaining the proposal. Your secondary action is to have the customer say, "I see you as a solution because your product meets my needs." Your primary action is to say, "Do you see us as a solution so that we can return to finalize our numbers and execute a contract? I want you to etch it somewhere in your brain that the sales cycle never changes once it's created.

What's coming up in Chapter 9? More hints and advanced selling facts, presented chapter and verse, that will help CSRs make the transition to a crack inside sales team capable of cross-selling. There will be more details about executing your sales plan and advice on how to overcome customer resistance and present your solution. Believe me, we're making good headway, but you might want to stand up and stretch a bit before continuing. "Mother, may I? Yes, you may."

9

"How Prepared Am I? So Prepared I Could Teach It!"

Developing a Sales Focus Before Presenting Solutions and Solving Problems

It may sound corny, but the Boy Scouts really have something with their years-old mantra, "Be Prepared." If you attained the level of Eagle Scout, well, then, you were expertly trained in preparation even before you traded in your olive green shorts for a navy blue pinstriped suit or comfortable pumps. I know this may sound like common sense to you, and if it does, congratulations, because then you know how many people lack common sense and don't understand why thorough preparation is vital no matter what goal you pursue.

Why Do You Need to Be Prepared?

In the world of competitive sales, preparation is especially critical because that factor can help differentiate you from others. It dictates your approach, gives you a solid foundation on which to build your sales plan, and can make the difference between success and failure. That's why I developed this entire concept to begin with. Selling is not a "quick on your feet" or "off the top of my head" type of process, although some of the most successful salespeople make it look that way. Believe me, these people have worked hard preparing their sales presentation materials, and if they're really smart they've been using my advanced consultative selling approach.

But like anything else you may have to learn—how to use a computer, the parameters of a new job, the rules of the road driving test, the contents of a professional test like the CPA exams—you need to review the materials and go over important elements over and over again until they become almost second nature. That's why I keep reviewing many of the selling details and strategies in nearly every chapter—so that you can strengthen your selling skills and eventually recite the process by rote. There's another reason, too. As I keep building in additional components to the half-quarter-half model, I'm also teaching how these skills fit in with the entire package and tie into one another and how many of the ACSR activities—presenting your solution, closing the sale—are built on these techniques. If you'd like, consider this as my version of an infomercial for advanced consultative selling. Except that you and your CSRs really have much more to gain by adopting these concepts and employing the tactics, and I guarantee you won't end up with an expensive, useless appliance. (For example, you really don't need that gizmo that helps you tighten your stomach muscles, even if you can make three easy payments. Just do stomach crunches. Trust me on this one.)

The Advantage of the Quarter-Half-Quarter Model

In my version of the sales approach that we've been discussing, careful preparation translates into creating a complete, yet adjustable sales plan, or what I like to call the critical path. Here we harken back to the all-important quarter-half-quarter model, which is designed to map out the sales process for you, guide your selling cycle, and help you map out your critical path.

One of the aspects I like about the quarter-half-quarter

model is that it's flexible and can be easily adapted to your company's product and the selling cycle you design for a particular customer. Remember, this is a circular model, resembling a clock face. You fill in the action steps as you proceed along the selling cycle. Most cycles contain between three and six steps, depending on your product. However, as we discussed earlier, before you begin filling in the blanks, it's important first to determine what your objectives will be each step of the way and how you're going to measure them when they happen. For example, the first sales approach or conversation with the customer may require three to five steps. Selling computer software may require only three steps, but computer hardware may take longer, as many as six or seven steps (Figure 9-1).

The flexibility part of the model, as well as the other major steps, assists you in your planning. Even though the basic actions of the model never change no matter what you're selling or whom you're selling to, the length of time spent on each quarter-half-quarter step may change, as may the intensity of each action. The number of steps in your particular sales cycle also dictate how you alter each movement and when. Again, these alterations also require preparation prior to each meeting or conversation with the customer. Don't worry that you might make a mistake, because a sales cycle (refer to Chapter 8) created according to the quarter-half-quarter map does not require a rocket scientist. It's directly tied to the product or service you're selling and the makeup of the customer company. This could be as simple as selling the customer one gizmo or fifteen.

It goes without saying that, as part of your preparation, you've learned everything about your own company's product by reading sales material, talking to the outside sales rep, talking to your product manager, and so on, so that you can capably ask the right questions as well as give correct information. Remember, once you get into the sales cycle, you'll be using the MLPQs to determine your customer's needs, so you'll have to understand what he's talking about in order to respond—and ask questions—intelligently. And as you advance, what kind of progress you make will determine when you move along in the quarter-half-quarter model.

Here's another way to look at it. Think of the process as a

Figure 9-1.   The action steps of a sales cycle.

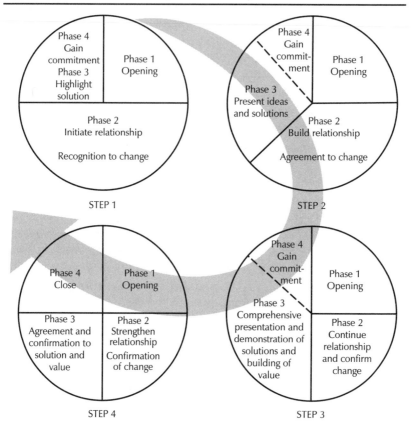

checkers game. You determine your moves ahead of time, but, depending on the player's actions, you may have to alter your prepared strategy. To win, you need to move in the most logical direction and know which moves will get you to the other side of the board. You must pay close attention and change your moves when it's necessary to meet your objections. King me!

Now let's look at another example, using a major health care product manufacturer's improved product. This sales cycle might take five steps to sell, say, your new line of baby formula when your target is already a customer for your sterile gloves. Before your CSR picks up the phone to make a call, this is the time to work out the anticipated sales plan. The CSR might call a pediatrician to talk with the office manager or head nurse to find out about their uses of baby formula, how they determine which formulas to distribute, how often they hand the formulas out, whether they charge anything for them, and whether there is any follow-up with the mothers.

From taking orders for sterile gloves let's assume that you, as the customer's CSR, already have a relationship with this manager or nurse. Now look at your quarter-half-quarter model and see that this action might take only one or two steps. Then move to the "half" portion of the model, asking questions and employing the MLPQ format. You might jump right to the agreement to change—one step. As it turns out, the office manager you've been speaking with is the decision maker, so she refers you to the pediatrician (the evaluator, according to the F.A.C.E. tactic we discussed in Chapter 8). Because she has already briefed him on the new baby formula and has related how it would fit in with the office's new-mother program, she is very receptive to your phone call. You jump to the next two steps— gaining commitment and presenting your solution—and you've made the sale.

Let's move this example into a different environment. Maybe you want to sell your new baby formula to a major pharmacy chain. Again, you have already established a relationship with a purchasing manager there through the sterile glove orders. You find out that the purchase decision is made by a committee, and, with the help of your friend the purchasing manager (your champion, remember?), you're referred to the decision maker of the committee. This particular cycle may take a couple of additional steps because you're dealing with a corporate bureaucracy, but you can still follow your model.

Please note that the F.A.C.E. tactic is an important component of the cycle. As you may recall, it's essential to identify the people who represent each role at the customer company. Remember that *F* stands for financial person, *A* stands for the appliers (the people who use the product), *C* is the champion, and *E* are the evaluators. And the better you cultivate your contact person, the quicker you'll be able to move through the cycle.

See how flexible this model can be? As your relationship matures and you make your way along the cycle, the emphasis moves along as well until you reach the last part of the cycle.

That means that your phone calls might move the quarter-half-quarter model into a quarter-quarter-half cycle, or a quarter-quarter-quarter cycle as you progress toward your goals. Then you can draft your proposal. Try practicing it. You'll see.

The Model and Time Management

There's another important component built into this sales cycle approach that you may have already noticed—time management. Most CSR departments tend to be understaffed these days, and CSRs already have their appointed duties—to help customers while answering phones—so it's even more important for these newly minted inside salespeople to closely manage their sales cycle times and be able to shift their gears quickly from the typical reactive duties to a more active stance. This certainly can pose a challenge for CSRs, but is not impossible, as long as management works with them. The CSR should begin with a list of about three items to cover and estimate how much time it will take. We're not talking about half-hour phone conversations, either. This isn't your mother. Neither the CSR nor the customer has time for that. A phone conversation may last only a few minutes, eventually taking about ten to fifteen minutes at the most. Each step of the way, following the quarter-half-quarter model, the CSR should lengthen the conversation by adding on to each step, especially when asking the multilayer questions. If the CSR properly captivates the customer with her line of questioning, she may end up shortening the allocated time.

The most important point for you to remember is that you need to be prepared for the inevitable. It's nice to know that intense preparation will actually pay off for you. It feels good, doesn't it, just knowing that you've reached the point you've been striving for? A friend of mine recently told me, with great pride, about her teenage daughter, who spent literally hours over several days trying to figure out an extremely complicated algebra equation—the kind the teacher gives out because he knows darn well that probably no one will be able to figure it out. During the school year, she's worked hard at learning this difficult subject. After all that work, she came up with the answer—the only one in the class to do so. My friend said she was beaming. I believe it.

Now it's your time to beam. After having moved through the quarter-half-quarter model's "half" section, asking questions and working through the funneling process, you've heard your customer say something like, "You know, what you've been saying makes a lot of sense to me. I think it's time for us to get rid of our old MIS equipment and look at how yours can save us time and money." A commitment to change.

Presenting the Solution—The Final Quarter

What do you do now that you've reached the moment you've been waiting for—presenting the solution? Remember, don't discard the information you've used in the other steps—especially what you learned in the final funneling process, because that's going to guide your solution. You've completed the first quarter and the half part of the quarter-half-quarter model, and now it's time to do what you like best—explain your product or service and sell it.

Completing the "half" signifies the development of a consultative relationship and the recognition of the need for change (Figure 9-2). Entering the last quarter allows you and your CSRs to present your solution to what was uncovered in the earlier funneling process during the "half" section of the model. As we discussed in Chapter 7, the final step of the funnel is the time to summarize what you've learned. For example, you might say, "As I understand it, Mr. Ball, you want distributors who offer just-in-time delivery, you're looking for a software program that will help you better manage inventory in your warehouse, and you want to consolidate the number of vendors you deal with." Your customer sighs, "Yes, but I don't know how I'm going to get it all done. I'll need some time to figure it all out." Eureka! The customer has acknowledged that there's a need for change. You execute your check/proceed technique—a finalizing action we'll discuss in Chapter 10 on overcoming objections—so that you can immediately move on to the final quarter. Because you'll be introducing the concept of benefit/feature selling, the

Figure 9-2.   The last quarter of the quarter-half-quarter model.

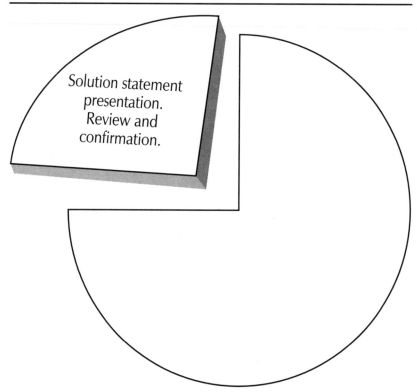

final quarter provides the guidelines for you and your CSR to distinguish and explain your solution to the customer.

Do you remember in Chapter 1 when my Toffler personality led you through the steps of a continuum, beginning at the "may I help you level," and moving up to a full-fledged ACSR (advanced customer services representative) level? At this point we're getting pretty close. Your CSRs are ready to enter the final phase of advanced consultative selling, having learned how to build relationships, ask information-collecting questions, prepare properly, and overcome roadblocks on their way to the sale.

The goal here is to enable you and your CSRs to clearly explain and present your product and service and describe what they mean to your customer. After all, you want to do a better job than your competitors. First, consider the following quote from Charles Revson, the former president of Revlon Cosmetics

Corporation, which I believe can put our efforts in perspective. When Revson was asked to describe his products, he responded: "In our factory we manufacture cosmetics; in the store we sell hope." What Revson was saying is that it's not the product or service that you are selling but what that product will do, how it will affect your customer, and how it will improve the issues you identified in the funnel.

The Three Steps in Making Your Presentation

I don't have to tell you, or your CSRs, that when presenting your product or service, it's important to make an effective presentation. After all, you're offering the customer a solution to his problems. I recommend adopting the following three-step process to make an effective presentation of your solutions. In this last quarter, the three steps in making effective presentations are:

Step 1: The solution statement
Step 2: The solution presentation
Step 3: The review and confirmation

Step 1: The Solution Statement

To illustrate Step 1, let me tell you a little story. It's time for your car's regular checkup. You take it into the shop, figuring the cost will be minimal because all the car needs is its state emission control sticker and an oil change. You're a fanatic about taking care of your car, so it's not only freshly waxed but has been running fine. When the phone rings later that morning in your office, it's Horace from the car repair shop. He says he's been working on your car and has a few questions for you. Have you been changing the oil regularly? Sure. What about the recommended tire rotation schedule? Sure, you've been sticking to that. Have you heard any funny noises when you break suddenly? No.

At this point, you're starting to get upset. You're thinking to yourself, what the heck is wrong with the car? How much is it going to cost to repair it? Do I need to get rid of it? Then Horace mumbles to you that the shop's computerized diagnostic system indicates there's a problem with the car. You begin to panic. The first thing you want to know is, What's the problem? Probably your next thought is, Can you fix it, or do I have to take it back to the dealer?

In this little vignette, your car seemed just fine with no bings or bangs; yet the shop mechanic diagnosed the car with a problem. You want an answer, and you want it now. Now let's switch gears to the selling situation. A similar plight has just happened to your customer. In the "half" part of the quarter-half-quarter model, you essentially diagnosed a problem, uncovered a need, and created the environment for change. Now the customer takes on the role of the panicked car owner. This is where you step in again. The purpose of the solution statement is to indicate to the customer that you have a solution to the woes that were uncovered during the funneling process. Why a solution statement? Because it can focus your customer's thought process as well as attest that you, indeed, have an answer that you are confident in and that has worked before. As teenagers say these days, "Been there, done that." Remember, people tend to make business decisions when the risk is minimal, and that's the message your solution statement is conveying.

Let me give you another illustration. Perhaps you know someone like this. He's an absolute health nut. For years he has always watched what he's eaten, hasn't smoked cigarettes, has exercised regularly, has gotten enough sleep, and has built his R&R (rest and relaxation) into his day. As part of his health consciousness, he also sees his doctor every year for his annual physical. As he's waiting in the doctor's office for the results, he's leaning back, musing how proud he is of his lifestyle. Even Oprah couldn't compare.

Finally, the doctor reappears, and he's got a funny look on his face. He tells him that after reviewing his test results, he has a few questions. Is he still exercising regularly? Yes. The doctor lets out one of those doctor-like acknowledgments. Hmmm. Still watching what you eat, avoiding red meat? Yes. The doctor— hmmm. The doctor leans over and, in a conspiratorial tone, asks,

"You're not smoking again, or abusing any drugs like alcohol or others, are you?" The health nut is offended. Of course not, he tells the doctor, his voice rising in pitch. Meanwhile, he's madly thinking to himself, What's going on? What's wrong with me? How could anything be wrong with me? Then, shaking his head, the doctor says to him, "I don't understand, but these test results suggest that you've got a problem." The health nut almost jumps out of his seat. "What is it? What's wrong with me? Can it be cured? Can you do it, or do I need another doctor? Whatever it is, I want to take care of it immediately."

This story is here to prove a point. With your customer, you have basically diagnosed a problem when you uncovered his needs and created a situation for his needs to be satisfied. From your client's point of view, depending on the situation, he may be feeling a bit anxious by what you've uncovered, so he'd like to move ahead quickly.

The Elements of the Solution Statement

It's up to you to meet his requirements and satisfy his concerns. That's why you use the solution statement. It consists of two elements—a *statement of confidence* and a *review of the benefits* your product or service provides that is based upon the information learned during the funneling process. This step allows you initially to assure the customer that you have the ability and the resources to offer a solution that meets his needs, just as at the car repair shop, once your car has been diagnosed, you want to know that there is a solution and that Horace can find the answer. In both cases, the person with the problem is looking for reassurance. With your client, your job is to put his mind at ease and let him know that you feel confident and that you're experienced at this process (even if you're not). These emotions can be conveyed over the phone by the tone of your voice. The solution statement and its elements fit into the framework of "Tell them what you're going to tell them, tell them, then tell them that you've told them" to reinforce your message.

The first part of the solution statement—*the statement of confidence*—carries enthusiasm along with your assertion of your belief in the product or service you are selling. It expresses your conviction about your product and your eagerness to offer a solution to your customer. Let me give you a more precise definition. Because selling is a transference of feeling, and people are motivated to change when risk is minimal (think about how small investors pour money into safer mutual funds when they don't really understand what's going on in the stock market), the solution statement is necessary to indicate your ability to perform and to gain the customer's attention and confidence. Combining the two elements of a confidence statement and benefit summary, you can initially assure your customer that you have the skills and the resources to provide a solution to his needs.

Think about advertisements you've seen that spell excitement, enthusiasm, and assurances that you're just going to love the product or service—fast-food hamburgers, specific car models, long-distance telephone services, a certain brand of candy that melts in your mouth and not in your hand (what a boast of confidence—try eating them on a hot day). These ads contain confidence statements. After all, if those marketers don't display confidence in their products, who will? (The trick, of course, is for the product to really deliver what it promises, but we'll save that for another day.)

The second part—*the benefit summary*—lists the appropriate benefits identified earlier during the funneling process that can be addressed by using your product and services as a solution to your customer's needs. For example, "Mr. Clinton, I am confident that our expertise in work station consolidation will help reduce expenses and increase work flow. Let me take a few minutes to explain how our Apollo system can address your key issues." Notice that this is a short and simple confirmation statement that allows you to address the customer's concerns, combined with a high level of confidence.

Remember my earlier story about buying a computer? I didn't tell you how we went about narrowing our search down to two models. The salesperson at the computer store really did a great job of determining our needs and then giving us a benefit summary, along with the computer's features. It was interesting to me to note that he used the funneling process, followed by his solution statement, followed by his confidence and benefit summary statements—whether or not he was aware of what he was doing. He touched on some very basic issues during his funneling process—how much we wanted to spend and how we planned to use the computer, for starters. Then he suggested that he show us a couple of models he thought could fulfill our needs.

Pointing to two different computers (he also turned them on and let us play with them a bit), he told us about the speed of the microprocessor and why that was important—did we want a 133 MHz or a faster model? He described the memory (would 16 RAM be enough?) and the hard-drive capacity (1.0 gigabytes is a whole lot of space). Then he summarized for us which combination would probably satisfy our needs, given our intended uses. I asked him about reliability. He promptly quoted from some computer magazines about how this manufacturer rated on reliability. Then he told me about the three-year warranty and that he had never heard a complaint about this computer manufacturer, giving us his solution statement and, then, finishing with the clincher—in fact, he had this model himself. In all, he used about four funnels in gathering information that was important to us and included his solution statement and confidence and benefit summaries.

He really sounded impressive to me. And of course I was keenly aware that his benefit summary—along with the computer's features, which we'll discuss more later—was a component of the solution statement. For a computer salesperson, benefit summaries are the critical part of the selling process. And, depending upon what you may be selling, it may be the same for you.

I realize that this computer illustration is a retail story, and a good salesperson of technology products should respond as this salesman did, but we can learn something from his approach. I believe it emphasizes how the solution statement and its confidence and benefit summaries work and why they're important to closing the sale. Why don't you try writing your own solution statement with a confidence assertion and benefit summary about your own product or service? Let me note here that you need not have a separate solution statement, confidence statement, and benefit summary. One sentence can do it all, if you create it carefully: for example, "Ms. Hurtz, I am confident that our expertise in computer technology will help you reduce your down time and meet your productivity requirements." This exercise will just take you a few minutes.

SOLUTION STATEMENT

_____

_____

CONFIDENCE STATEMENT/BENEFIT SUMMARY

_____

_____

_____

Step 2: The Solution Presentation

The second step, presenting your company and solution, is really the heart of this chapter, because this is the step where you give the customer a complete explanation of the benefits and features of your product/service and what they mean to the customer. Throughout this book, we've introduced and discussed a series of building blocks designed to lead you to fashion a relationship with your customer and welcome her acknowledgment for change, so all that's left to do is sell your solution with the right kind of pizzazz. Pay especially close attention to this step, because it is here that you organize your solution presentation so that you can clearly demonstrate your ability to solve the customer's problem and distinguish yourself from the other companies.

Benefit/Feature Selling

Effective presentations are centered on the concept of benefit/feature selling. In and of itself, this concept is not new, but how we're going to use it is new. As Charles Revson reminded us, truly successful salespeople and executives sell benefits, not specific products or services. CSRs need to know that benefit selling motivates customers to buy and provides a clear explanation of how a salesperson's services offer a solution to their needs. When presenting your product or service it's important to identify what your product or services provide for the customer, on the basis of what you learned in your earlier funneling.

Let me give you another example. You probably know dozens of people who, for different reasons, have decided to open up their own consulting businesses. Sometimes they've been laid off (or downsized; you pick), were unhappy at their jobs and couldn't find something better, or simply decided it was time to strike out on their own. One associate in particular naively figured it would be simple to buy a computer, have some business cards printed, install a phone, and go into business. He learned the hard way that it's not so easy. When he started calling old business associates looking for consulting work, they were friendly but basically futured him by telling him cheerfully it was great to catch up and when they had some business he would be the first one they would call. When the phone didn't ring, he wondered what he was doing wrong.

After six months of watching him agonize, I finally suggested we have lunch and talk about his business. I must admit I was pretty frank with him, but I was sure I could offer him some helpful advice. I began by asking him a lot of question—dialogue and MLPQs, if I recall. After several funnels, I offered him my thoughts. As it turned out, as a financial expert, he was billing himself as all things to all people. He assumed that because he had several years of financial experience with several corporations, people would realize the benefits of hiring him. But that was obviously not the case.

He decided to focus on one particular area that, from his experience, he knew many companies struggled with. He knew the ups and downs of that issue and how typical corporate financial departments always let it go by the wayside. But he was good at that task and rather enjoyed doing it, so he knew that (1) he was skilled to handle it, (2) he was enthusiastic, (3) he understood how it fit into the entire scheme of a financial department, (4) he could accurately handle the assignment in a relatively short period of time and free up other employees to complete other tasks.

He sent letters to financial department heads, outlining the benefits of hiring an outside consultant to handle that particular assignment. He sent out six letters and received six responses. He later told me he had gone in for several interviews and made a point of assessing the company's specific needs. That was several months ago, and the last time I called him he said he was too busy to talk but noted that he now had eight steady clients and that two of them had already assigned him some additional tasks, as well. In fact, he was getting so busy he was thinking about moving out of his home office, leasing office space, and hiring an assistant. And, no, I didn't send him a bill, but he did treat me to a very nice dinner.

Now, let's take a second look at this story. My friend was floundering in his efforts to get his new consulting business off the ground until he began pitching potential clients the benefits and features they could realize by hiring him. His benefits included completing the tasks in question in a short period of time, thus contributing to the department's productivity while costing the company less than a full-time employee. One benefit of hiring him was the freeing up of other employees for other assignments; he was also very experienced at executing the project in question, as well as others that might come his way. I'm pleased that it has turned out so well for him.

I define benefits as those actions that stem from the use of your products or services. They support what you are offering as a solution to your customer's needs. Try comparing benefits with something else that is intangible, that you can't physically grab and hold on to. For example, try describing your best friend by using only characteristics that are intangible; for me, I came up with "honest," "classy," "humorous," and "intelligent." For the service or product you're selling, common benefits are improved quality, improved productivity, lower cost, better performance, and greater safety. Like your friend's characteristics, you can't hold these benefits in your hand, but they certainly can support your product or service.

Let's face it. Almost every salesperson says he's selling a quality product that will improve the customer's bottom line. So why shouldn't your customer think that you're offering just some more empty promises? Here's what you'll do differently:

1. State the benefit.
2. State the selling features.
3. Explain the features in detail to make them understandable.
4. Show how and why this results in an advantage to the prospect.
5. Link every feature to a benefit using the information derived from the funnels (e.g., "and this means you can save thousands of dollars or reduce your labor costs").

Generally speaking,

- Every presentation should contain several benefits.
- Every benefit should be supported by at least three features.
- Features can support more than one benefit.

As I said earlier, you're going to tell them what you're going to tell them, then tell them, then tell them what you told them. Your job is to bring these benefits and features to life and make them believable to the customer by describing the features of your product in an exciting and passionate manner. Features are the specific characteristics of your product or service. They're the tangible elements that explain how your product is built and operates or communicate how a service is provided. Remember, you may know your product backwards and forwards, but your client doesn't. Don't assume that product attributes that seem simple and apparent to you don't need to be stated or illustrated.

In addition to benefits and features, one other characteristic can separate your approach to benefit/feature selling and your competition's. I call it the "advantage." Pointing out the advantage of your service or product really is the frosting on the cake. It's a piece of information, or several pieces of information, about how your product or service meets the customer's needs that your competitors don't have but that you do, because you can tie your benefits/features back to the funneling process. Remember, you already know what issues are important to your customer thanks to your funnels. Maybe it's safety. Maybe it's productivity. These customer concerns put you ahead of the game because they reflect what the customer wants done. Your competition doesn't know that. As one insurance ad has been saying for years, "Get the advantage." I'll return to this concept a bit later.

It's test time again, folks, to assure yourself that these concepts are really sinking in. Before we begin, I'll run down the basic definition of benefits, features, and advantages for you in direct terms:

- Benefit—What is derived from the use of your service that indicates a solution to the customer's needs
- Feature—A characteristic of your service or product
- Advantage—Translation of your benefit/feature and the way it addresses the need of the customer

OK. Now it's your turn.

DISTINGUISHING FEATURES AND BENEFITS

Each of the following three statements contain a feature and a benefit. Please reach each statement carefully and identify the benefit, feature, and advantage in the appropriate spaces.

1. Commercial Service   "Our commercial refrigeration service contract means lower cost in use to you, Mr. March, because our monthly inspection and schedule maintenance is less costly than emergency repair resulting from inadequate or improper servicing."

Feature: _____

Benefit: _____

Advantage: _____

2. Insurance   "This policy, Ms. Stitch, features a
                            waiver of premium in the event of
                            an illness or accident. This means
                            greater peace of mind because, if
                            you should be laid up for more
                            than six months, you will not have
                            any premium payments."

Feature: _____

Benefit: _____

Advantage: _____

3. Banking   "The twenty-four-hour inquiry ser-
                            vice makes it easy to keep accurate
                            track of your funds and make
                            transfers without coming to the
                            bank."

Feature: _____

Benefit: _____

Advantage: _____

How did you do? In the first question, on commercial service, the feature is that the service contract means a monthly
inspection. The benefit is the lower cost. The advantage is that
there is no inadequate or improper servicing. In the second
question, on insurance, the feature is the waiver of premium, the
benefit is greater peace of mind, and the advantage is no pre-

mium payments. For the third question, on banking, the feature is twenty-four-hour-service, the benefit is accurate tracking of funds, and the advantage is the convenience of not having to make a trip to the bank.

I realize that sometimes it's tough to remember which definition is which, so maybe keeping one of these more simplified examples in mind will help.

The sales trainer at MCI Corporation, Andy Trackman, at one time described to me how the company's shift to CSR selling has not only been a boost to sales but has also aided the company in selling the benefits and features of several of its products, because the CSRs themselves use more high-tech products themselves. Following a client meeting, it used to take the sales force a week to ten days to get follow-up letters out to the customers. But when the salespeople began using laptop computers, they could generate letters immediately after meetings answer customers' questions right away. As a bonus, the company's receivables improved because of this automation. It seems logical that, if a customer was in the market for some kind of advanced communication product and needed to speed up its sales force's client response time and to improve receivables, the client would be impressed with this hands-on illustration of MCI's confidence, experience, and ability to understand and use its own advanced products.

Of course, not every salesperson can capitalize on this type of selling situation. More often, you have to work a bit harder to illustrate the benefits and features of your product line. I know that most salespeople are familiar with benefit/feature selling because the concept itself has been around for many years. The approach has stood the test of time because it acts as a template to help salespeople effectively make a presentation and explain how their products or services work.

The Impact of Product Parity on the Marketplace

Unfortunately, benefit/feature selling by itself frequently fails because so many salespeople use the same approach in their presentations; also, many of today's products are in many ways interchangeable. Isn't one computer just like another?

Don't lots of people look at computer makers that way? What about telephone systems? That's why benefit/feature selling is no longer sufficient to move the customer to truly understand the superiority of your product or service and to make that buying decision.

Years ago, when I worked for a large company, I participated in a training session on the newfangled phone system the company was installing. When the trainer directed us to pick up our voice modules, I couldn't believe it. To me it looked just like a phone.

Then, recently, as I shopped for a new office telephone system, that experience ran through my mind as I listened to the salesperson describe a new phone system to me. He asked me how we intended to use the system and what we wanted it to do. He asked me what our biggest problem with our current system was and pointed out to me maintenance records of the different systems. Because my business lives and dies by the telephone, I chose the system with the easiest maintenance records, the fewest problems, and features that could adjust to our growing business needs. Looking back, I was probably a nightmare customer because I was carefully listening for the steps of his selling cycle and probably not paying as close attention to what he was actually telling me. Goodness knows how many times I had to say, "I'm sorry. Could you repeat that, please?"

I'm not exactly certain why I chose this particular phone system, except that I was getting ready to leave town and I wanted to get it over with. This demonstrates why it's important to pay attention not only to the customer's corporate needs but also to his situation while you're talking to him. Maybe he sounds rushed because he is, so focus on your most important benefits/features, because you may not have time to go into more detail.

One of the reasons I told you this story is that it relates to how you need to overcome product parity in the marketplace—a phone system is a phone system is a phone system—for your product or service and make your benefit/features stand out above the crowd. Why not add another element, such as "the advantage"? (Imagine a big, bold voice saying this, and it has more impact.) The advantage is simply the translation of how your benefits and features address and solve the issues identified during the funneling process. Tying the benefit/feature selling process to the funnels is what makes this traditional technique work. Without tying the information back to the funnels, your presentation is simply just another presentation of information and numbers that don't relate to what the customer really wants done.

At the risk of repeating myself, benefits are intangible and can't be touched; features are tangible. Think of them as a table: The benefit acts as the table top, and the features are the legs. With only one or two legs, the table falls over, but with three, four, or more legs the table has solid support and will withstand heavy weight and abuse. The same is true of your presentation.

By now, you can probably recite from rote memory the definitions of benefit/feature/advantage selling. Just to be sure, pick up your pencils again, and have your CSRs pick up a pencil, too, and write down the definitions of a benefit, a feature, and an advantage. If you wrote that a benefit refers to how a customer uses your product, a feature is a specific characteristic, and an advantage is how your feature and benefit are tied back to the information you found out in the funneling process, then you win (sorry, no actual prizes are available).

What Do Customers Really Want?

Now you need to figure out what the actual benefits/features/advantages are of your own products or services. To do this, it helps to study the purchasing patterns of individuals, and I have just the device to assist us. In the last several years my firm has conducted an ongoing informal study of the thousands of people who attend my seminars, asking how an individual purchases a product or service. We have surveyed more than 10,000 people, and I think you'll agree that the results are quite intriguing. We were looking at buying habits that could be measured and repeated, using the premise of a customer looking to purchase a refrigerator, since most people have had to buy one at some time in their lives. The participants in the survey were asked what they look for when buying a refrigerator. To no one's surprise, the list included ice makers, ice water dispensers, movable shelves, side-by-side doors, and energy efficiency—what we call values, as in value for the money.

When we wanted to reduce the list of refrigerators to three choices, the participants listed quality as their first criterion, eliminating the brands that did not have a reputation for quality. Then, to reduce the list further, we gave them another choice of criteria, asking whether the remaining three refrigerators would be able to offer both the conveniences and the desired price. For this question, all the respondents agreed that value was the second most important element governing their selection, defining value as providing the most use for the money. They then reduced the list to two possible choices.

To determine their preferred choice, participants were asked to select from one of the two choices on the basis of which manufacturer had the best customer service and support when needed. Based upon this criterion, all of the participants selected their preferred refrigerators.

I can hear you now scratching your heads, wondering how this research on buying refrigerators relates to the products and services you sell. Actually, the correlation is very strong. As a result of this survey, we learned that the majority of individuals look first for quality, then for value, and finally for reliability or support from the product maker. With the majority of 10,000 respondents indicating that this is how they make a significant purchase, we concluded that this is probably how most individuals make purchase decisions. (That's how I decided to buy my office telephone system.) Following this premise, if individuals buy quality, value, and reliability, it makes sense to organize your presentation to your customers in the same manner.

Defining Quality, Value, and Reliability

When presenting your benefits, *quality* should be your first point, *value* should be your second, and *reliability* should be your third. Let's take a second look at value for a minute. Consider the funneling process again. Whatever is identified in the funneling process during the half part of the model are the benefits that you will categorize under the value section of your presen-

tation. Your value-added benefits should be sandwiched between the benefits of quality and reliability.

How do you define *quality?* When you're selling a service,
this benefit relates to the talents, expertise, and knowledge of
those who perform or design the service that's being sold, including education and awards. If you're selling a product, focus
upon how a product is made, tested, designed, researched; the
material used; patents held; and procedures for meeting quality
control standards. Remember our discussion on tangibles and
intangibles? When selling a tangible item, focus on how it is
built and tested. When selling an intangible item, focus on the
talents, expertise, and knowledge of those who perform or design the service.

Now let's examine *value.* This category of benefits is very
broad, but, in a nutshell, your customer is looking to reduce
something or increase something. He may want to reduce his
cost, overtime, downtime, or returns. He may want to increase
sales, performance, or customer satisfaction. Any of these, and
more, will work for your presentation as long as they're related
to the funneling process. If the customer wants to increase performance and at the same time lower costs, then these are the
two value benefits that you need to present. No more, no less—
just what was identified in the funnels. Let me offer you a word
of caution here for you as well as your CSRs. This "no more, no
less" rule seems to often challenge salespeople who can get carried away when they describe their product or service and what
it can do. Please avoid the temptation of trying to sell everything
to the customer or to oversell. The customer wants only to meet
his needs, solve his problems, and learn about how your product
and service can do it best.

Here's another example. Let's say you're a 38-year-old bachelor—I'll call you Darryl from Chicago—who wants to buy that
ultimate 38-year-old bachelor status car—a Mercedes (at least,
that's what I'd buy if I were a 38-year-old bachelor). You walk
into the auto showroom, look around at the glistening cars, and
tell the salesperson who approaches you, "I'm a tall man. I want
to make sure that my head clears the ceiling easily, and that the
two front seats are comfortable and convenient. I don't care
about the back seats at all." The salesperson nods his head, as if

he understands perfectly. Then he proceeds to walk over to a four-door model, open the back door and begin waxing eloquent about the increased leg room. He even gets in the car to demonstrate.

But didn't you tell the salesperson that the backseat was unimportant to you? That it has no value for you? Besides, people tend to be wary of packaged prices because they might include unwanted features, and, as a result, may be higher priced. So the moral of this Mercedes: although the feature may be a nice thing to have and could be beneficial to some people, if Darrell from Chicago or another particular customer doesn't want to pay for it, it has no value to him. That's why I stress again—no more, no less.

Here's an example. Recently, my wife and I decided we wanted to buy a treadmill for our home. All I really cared about was the speed, which translated into how much horsepower the treadmill had. I wanted it to be able to go fast enough so I could really run on it. Meanwhile, Annette, who was going to use the treadmill, too, was concerned about too much horsepower. She thought it could be dangerous. I explained this to the store salesman.

He nodded his head, and, after explaining how to get the speed (the 2.5 horsepower motor), he proceeded to tell us about the precision design, the longer-life two-ply belt, the built-in circuit breakers, the welded aircraft-grade aluminum alloy frame, the permanently lubricated bearings, and on and on. My wife interrupted him and asked, "Yes, I understand it's got these other features, too, but does it have the quality we wanted?" I must say, the entire time he was talking, I was just shaking my head, knowing he was going overboard, telling us things we really didn't care about. He obviously felt compelled to give me at least three to four features to convince me of the quality of the treadmill. As we walked out of the store, Annette, chuckling, asked me if I could recite all the treadmill's features. I looked her straight in the eye and said, "I remember one. It's got what I want."

I hope you understand now why I stress no more, no less, and how important that funneling process really is so that you know what features and benefits are truly important to the customer. We didn't care about the treadmill's construction and belt. We just wanted it to run fast and safely. The salesperson could have saved himself a lot of time if he knew the process.

Take a look at the following list of value benefits that you might consider for your product or service. Remember, value benefits translate into dollars. They include:

- Increased efficiency
- Increased sales
- Increased production continuity
- Increased protection of contract
- Less turnovers
- Lower maintenance costs
- Increased space savings
- Lower labor costs
- Less downtime
- Lower initial costs
- Lower cost in use

Now let's move on to the next point identified by the participants in the survey—*reliability.* This refers to your company's reputation and services. In your presentation, you might want to use the expression such as "greater peace of mind." It's also important that you provide proof for your claims. Why not be creative? Appeal to all of the senses. The CSRs can try to paint a picture in the customer's mind. By all means, mention testimonials, test data, and the results of surveys. Just remember to start with quality and end with reliability, sandwiching your value-added elements—what comes out of the funnels—in the middle.

I've developed a manageable form that will help you distinguish your benefits and features for your customer. (I tried it out on my grade-school son, and he thought it looked easy.) To repeat, a benefit is what the customer purchases. It is the end result of what your product or service does for him. The feature is an element of a design, construction, or service facility that enables your product or service to deliver that benefit. Now, keep our goal in mind, to make the most effective presentation, as you review the following caveats for filling out the form:

■ The average product or service should have no fewer than three benefits and no more than five. Where possible, combine two similar benefits, such as greater efficiency and greater productivity, under one subject heading. You need at least three to make it substantial and believable, but no more than five because that becomes overwhelming for the customer.

■ Every benefit must have at least three features. For example, a benefit providing lower cost might have features such as ways to lower maintenance expenses, methods for getting the job done quicker, and lower initial price.

■ Try to keep the benefits in sequence. Start off with benefits that relate to quality, followed by value and reliability benefits (remember our sandwich analogy).

■ A single feature may be used two or three times to substantiate a benefit.

Good luck with filling out your form. If you'd like a few minutes to practice by filling it out off the top of your head, by all means do so.

Please identify, in order of importance, your company's top benefits:

1. _____   _____

                                  _____

                                  _____

                                  _____

2. _____   _____

                                  _____

                                  _____

                                  _____

3. _____   _____

                                    _____

                                    _____

                                    _____

4. _____   _____

                                    _____

                                    _____

                                    _____

5. _____   _____

                                    _____

                                    _____

                                    _____

This is how I would have filled out this form. The left side is for your benefits; Number 1 is quality, number 2, 3, and 4 are values that have come out of your funnel, and number 5 is reliability. The spaces on the right side should contain your features for each category.

An example of quality is "Our staff developed this technology, and we're the leading provider to the federal government." Values, which you derived from the funnels, are key issues that translate into dollars, such as "Our technology has proven to be the most efficient, improving productivity while lowering operating costs. In fact, certain arms of the federal government have adopted our technology." And, reliability is reflected in statements such as "Due to our regular maintenance program you can be assured that this system will never break down, offering you greater peace of mind for your operations."

Notice that I left only a limited number of spaces for you to identify your company benefits, so you don't end up overwhelming your customer with information she may not need or remember. For example, let's say the day after your conversation with your customer, she happens to be talking to her partner and mentions your new product conversation. She tells her partner that it looks like it offers the value, benefits, and reliability that she would want, but she's really not able to recite each feature. Her partner asks her to give her some examples. The customer may be able to remember only a few, so that's all you need to really give her.

Now we've reached the third step of the final quarter.

Step Three: The Review and Confirmation

As the final step in your presentation, review the key issues, review the benefits, and look for confirmation of the benefits and solutions. More specifically, you should:

- Review the key issues—the needs outlined in the first half—and how your benefits/features address those needs and offer a solution.
- Seek confirmation that the prospect accepts and acknowledges your solution and presentation.

What you're looking for is the client's acknowledgment of acceptance, agreement, and commitment. If you'd like, think of this as AAC. To get her response, try something like this: "Ms. Jones, throughout our conversation, you've mentioned your concern about the impact on your company of the new Medicare changes. I know that our expertise in health care accounting and the new federal health rules that I've demonstrated to you will be able to put your mind at ease. On the basis of our discussion, are you confident that we have the expertise and resources to restructure your Medicare billings and flesh out any cost reductions that are available? Is there anything else I haven't made clear to you?"

Acquiring acceptance, agreement, and commitment to your conversation's primary objective is relatively easy once you've gotten the confirmation from the customer. Let's try another test to help you draft your own summary statements:

Key Issues:

_____

_____

_____

_____

Benefit Review:

_____

_____

_____

_____

Confirm:

_____

_____

_____

_____

If you prefer, you can use the example of Medicare, or you can simply use your own examples.

Your CSR's next step is to go from commitment to action. "Because you agree that my firm's specialty in health care accounting and federal programs can ensure that the BetterHealth Company complies with the new rules, I'd like to arrange a formal presentation to your company management committee," or "submit a proposal," or "have you visit our facility and meet our experts," or "meet your president," or "sign a contract." Once you've gotten an agreement, you need to move on to the next step of your cycle.

Practicing Your Solution Presentation

Now it's your turn to develop a scenario that incorporates all the major points we've gone through this chapter, using information presented in earlier chapters. Let me give you some tips firsts. To verify your benefits, say to yourself, "I have to state the features," then say, "this means . . . ," and state the benefit. Remember my treadmill story? The treadmill was made out of aluminum, and "this means greater quality." Stay away from saying anything like "it was made in the United States," or "we have been in business for twenty years." That may indicate pride and longevity and give the impression of quality, but it doesn't really document quality, and that's what you're trying to do. Remember, also, a feature can support different benefits and can be used over and over again—the aluminum means less maintenance and longer life.

Now pick a product or service that you are familiar with. Replay a conversation with a sales rep starting the conversation with "I'm confident. . . ." Describe the product's benefits or features, perhaps relying on your benefit/feature form that you worked with earlier. Complete the sales rep/customer dialogue with some variation of the closing statements just mentioned. Now read it through again. Are you comfortable with it? If not, make whatever changes are necessary until you feel comfortable that the customer would have no choice but to give a resounding yes.

Congratulations. You're almost there. Because, unfortunately, no presentation goes perfectly smoothly, in Chapter 10 I'm going to discuss how to overcome resistance and objections. So, stay tuned.

10

"No, Thank You, I'm Just Looking"

Overcoming Resistance and Objections

I'm going to begin this chapter with an easy test. I guarantee you, unlike some of the others, it won't tax your brains too much. Here goes:

1. What's your favorite color?
2. What's your favorite flower?
3. What's your favorite piece of furniture?
4. What's your favorite animal in the zoo?
5. Pick a whole number between zero and five, including five.

Every time I give a seminar, I begin this topic with these questions. The most frequently given responses are (1) blue, (2) rose, (3) couch or sofa, (4) lion or tiger, (5) three and four. The point of this exercise is simple. We're all pretty predictable about our responses to certain kinds of questions. The same applies to our customers. Seasoned salespeople can confirm that there are also only four or five objections that we typically hear from customers, and most salespeople have heard them many times. CSRs are likely to hear these common objections as well. Do you know what they are?

"It costs too much," or "Your price is too high."
"I'm satisfied with my current vendor."
"It doesn't meet my needs."
"It's not in our budget."
"We've had a bad experience with your company in the past."

If I were to take a scientific survey of all the salespeople in the country, I'm certain these customer responses would rank right up there as the most common responses they hear. But these responses may be new to you CSRs, and I certainly don't want to see you stopped dead in your tracks when a prospect spouts one of these phrases. That's what this chapter examines—how to anticipate negative customer responses and learn how to overcome them in a gracious yet assertive manner. After all, it's not as if objecting to a question were a new concept for you. People do it almost every day. And there are certainly degrees of objection; some are easier to deal with than others. Consider this recent personal experience.

I'm not really keen on shopping. It's not that I don't like buying new stuff. It's just that salespeople drive me nuts. Not long ago I was shopping around for a 4×4 sport utility vehicle, and I'm the type who studies the dealership ads looking for the best buy for the money that will fit my needs. I decided to test-drive some of these utility vehicles, even though I already had an idea of which one I wanted. So what happened the minute I stepped foot into a dealer showroom? I was approached by a pleasant salesperson who asked me, "Can I help you with a new car?" to which I responded, "No, thanks, I'm just looking."

"Just looking" is a natural response to a salesperson, even though I knew I was a serious buyer (I was really drooling over this car), and the salesperson's experience told her that I was probably qualified, too. But I still essentially told her to go away. Why did I do that? Simple. Because anytime a salesperson asks you some version of "can I help you," your natural, immediate response is no, even though you may actually be very interested. In short, all of us register some kind of objection when placed in the buying mode. Perhaps we object because we're not ready to buy yet, don't realize the need for it, or have to discuss the purchase with others first. The "just looking" response can happen anytime during the sales process, but it's most common at the beginning.

Consider this example. In most towns, real estate agents frequently hold what are known as "open houses," usually on Sunday afternoons, to draw attention to the homes that are on the market and to get as many people as possible to view them, hoping some looker will want to buy. The real estate agents I've spoken with tell me that typically most of the people visiting the open houses are true house seekers, although they may not end up buying those particular homes. When approached, they'll give the most common response—"Just looking." On the other hand, many people do end up buying the house they first see at an open house.

Still, I feel obligated to mention a friend of mine who loves to go to open houses, especially those in her neighborhood, to get decorating ideas and to see how the prices of the homes compare with the value of her house. Similarly, some people really are just car junkies and are truly "just looking" when they visit an auto dealership. But often, the customers really were going to buy even though, initially, they indicated they weren't really interested.

Let's transfer this discussion to the CSR's experience with questioning and listening to the customer, helping her to acknowledge the need for change, offering the solution, and making the sale. What did that car salesperson have to do to get my attention and turn my objection into a sales solution? She didn't know the techniques contained in this chapter (fortunately for her, I really wanted that 4 × 4), but let's try spelling them out to help you CSRs learn how to overcome objections. Remember, objections are a natural part of the sales process. Even our colleagues and management staff raise objections from time to time. In fact, come to think of it, so do my family, colleagues, and friends. But no salesperson should take them personally because the objections are targeted toward what the CSR represents—the product, service, or ideas. The customer isn't saying you're a bad person but is simply registering a resistance to change. And as the seller, you have to learn to anticipate this resistance, because some aspect of it will probably be there, even if your customer does want to buy your service or product. As a business associate once told me, "I have to give the salesperson some resistance, even if I do intend to buy his product, just to keep him honest."

This point is crucial for the CSR to take to heart, because it's probably one of the biggest downfalls of salespersons. Once you understand that, it's much easier to proceed. Unfortunately, more often than not, customers voice objections, and it's not easy to overcome that challenge and persuade the customers to realize a need for change, especially when they have been satisfied with a competing product or service, or to see a need for what you represent. That's what this chapter addresses. By the way, have a pencil nearby, too.

Objections occur before a person becomes a customer. Objections register initial resistance to what you are explaining and/or representing and may arise anywhere in the sales cycle.

With that in mind, let's look at the CSRs' demeanor and approach. How would you handle objections? Try these criteria on for size:

- Understand the customer's point of view.
- Be relaxed when responding.
- Encourage the customer to talk.
- Establish an atmosphere of problem solving.
- Listen.
- Maintain poise and confidence.
- Be polite; speak clearly.
- Recognize that the customer is objecting not to you as an individual but to your position.
- Take a consultative, nonadversarial approach.

Do you use these measures? Now let's look at what we can expect from the client. As I said before, objections can arise anytime during the sales process—during the opening of the sales conversation, while you're uncovering the customer's needs and seeking change, or even when you're presenting your solutions and trying to gain a commitment. I'm sure veteran salespeople are familiar with hearing, "Your price is too high," "You don't have the technology, resources, or availability that we are looking for," "I deal with you only about xxxxx," and the classic "I'm satisfied with my present supplier." Some could read these objections as some sort of an indictment of what they're trying to accomplish, but that's not accurate. An objection shouldn't throw you off course and cause you to babble to the customer. That's why it's important to be prepared to counter these objections with some well-defined strategies.

I created a concise set of strategies, known as the Four-Step Process, to help you deflect almost any objection and regain control of the sales call. The four steps are Neutralize, Question, Resolve, and Check/Proceed.

Neutralize

The first step, *neutralize*, is actually a two-part process. When you note an objection, pause for a few minutes. Do nothing. Count to two. This tactic gives you an opportunity to think before you respond and avoid blurting out an answer that may not be appropriate. Meanwhile, the client gets the impression that your response was not prepackaged and that you take his objections seriously. But don't wait as long as ten seconds, because to the customer it seems like an uncomfortable pause that lasts a lifetime, and he may think you haven't been listening. On the other hand, if you respond with an immediate answer or solution, you run the risk of creating an adversarial situation as well as losing an opportunity to learn more about the client's perspective. A couple of seconds is just right. If you don't answer objections when they are first registered, instead, acknowledge the client's statement and encourage dialogue. This tells the customer of your interest in hearing his thoughts.

The major thrust of this step is to neutralize what the sales prospect has said. If you're any kind of science fiction fan—say, a *Star Trek* fanatic—it conjures up images of a particular episode when the enemy (the Borg) says it's going to "neutralize" Captain Jean Luc and the crew. However, in your case, you're not going to eliminate your client just because he makes an objection (but it's tempting, right?). Instead, in this version of neutralizing, you are going to convert him from his way of thinking to yours. If someone is neutral, she doesn't have an opinion one way or another. Neutral means sitting in the middle. And that's what you will be striving to be with your remarks—they will be neutral when responding to your customer's objections—initially, that is.

To do this, you simply agree—the second part of the neutralizing concept—with the major concept of the customer's statement without actually agreeing with what was really said. Your agreement statement is important because it positions you in an unchallenged state and enables you to solicit the opinion of the client about the situation. Maybe your customer has said many times that she's satisfied with XYZ Company or has made another counterpoint to your discussion that requires neutralization. If you've had any prior training experience—selling, customer service, marriage compatibility, conflict resolution— you've learned that if you're at opposite sides of an issue with someone else, the worst thing you can say is, "You're wrong." A more generic but very usable lead-in phrase could be, "I can understand how you can feel that way"; then you continue your specific statement. Please don't be tempted to tell your customer she's wrong about her current vendor or end up supporting your competition by using the wrong lead-in statement such as these:

> **Her remark:** "I'm very satisfied with my vendor."
> **Your response:** "Yes, they are a good company." (supports the competition)
> "What do you like about what they do?" (supports competition)
> "Yes, they are a good company, but. . . ." (telling customer she's wrong)

Do you understand why these responses won't further your own efforts? If the customer does allude to being happy with her current supplier, don't respond by saying something like, "Yes, they are a good company, but . . ." because you're telling her that her assessment of the competition is inaccurate, and you could end up insulting the customer. And I believe you can understand why the other two phrases agreeing that the competition is a good company and asking her to review what appeals to her about the competition is self-defeating. That's why you need to neutralize her remarks. So if she says she's happy with XYZ Company because it offers good service, reliability, and maybe a fair price, you can agree with the essence of what she said by noting, "Yes, good service, reliability, and value are certainly essential," adding, "What do you look for in those areas?" If the customer answers the questions, where's the objection? It disappeared. Remember, you need to agree with the concept of the statement and not the exact statement itself.

Let's try it again. Should the prospect say that your company is too big, the neutralizing statement could be, "Receiving the proper attention and response is certainly important." Then it's your turn to deflect the conversation to an issue you can control. How? If you answer this correctly, you win the $64,000 question. The answer is: Use the issues you identified from the funneling process. Remember, the funnels are where you identified the major issues for the customer, setting the stage for future questioning. Did you answer my question correctly? If so, you win—and I'll pay you when I win the lottery. Returning to the funnels—let's say you have a funnel that has service, reliability, and value at the top, and the bottom represents change. At least one of the features listed in the funnel would be "expanding into other areas." These represent what makes somebody satisfied. To make your neutralizing statement work, you have to first identify these issues.

Here's an example. Let's say your spouse complains to you one evening that "you're never home." (Sounds familiar to some readers, huh?) If you respond, "You're right," you're admitting your guilt, while, in essence, your spouse is saying, "I miss you, and you're not around to carry your weight." If you're smart, you'll say, "Spending time together is important." But did you say you'd be home more often? No. So even though there's really an indictment here, you've successfully deflected the conversation to something you can control. What you could say, instead, is, "Knowing our schedules, how can we make this happen?" (Much better.) Not only do you neutralize your spouse's anger, but you pick up the funneling issues that are important to your spouse and address them in a question that leads to further conversation.

Question

The second step in overcoming customer objections is to question further the customer's statements. Sample questions are "What do you look for in a relationship?" and "What are your expectations?" Done properly, you can temporarily ward off the objections because when the client is answering your question, he is focusing on another issue. And this opens the door for you to present your ideas. As you should throughout this entire process, you should rely on your questioning criteria, such as dialogue-probing (I'll go into more detail on this later). But if you can successfully neutralize the customer's objections by pausing, agreeing, and asking the right questions, you don't need to use Steps 3 and 4, because you'll have already addressed and solved the problem. In a sense, Step 1 and Step 2 can never be separated (Figure 10-1).

Figure 10-1.   Step 1 and Step 2 in overcoming objections.

```
┌─────────────────────────┐
│                         │
│   Step 1   Neutralize    │
│                         │
│   Step 2   Question      │
│                         │
└─────────────────────────┘
```

Let's see how you're doing so far. In the next exercise, mark the best neutralizing response to common customer objections.

Doesn't meet my need:

_____ Meeting your needs is important. In what way does our service not meet your needs?

_____ Providing the right solution for your situation is essential. What are the key elements you look for?

_____ Satisfaction is important. What do the other products have that we don't?

_____ Looking at our solution, what do we offer that does meet your needs?

I'm satisfied with my vendor:

____ I'm glad to hear you're happy. What is it that you like?
____ Many of our clients are satisfied as well. Let me tell you what we have done for others.
____ Quality, value, and service are important. Tell me what you look for.
____ Tell me whom you are dealing with.

Your prices are too high:

____ How much is too high?
____ If we could lower our price, could we then begin the work?
____ Getting the best value and business insight from your vendor in the long term is important. Do you mind if I ask you a few questions?
____ We provide top-quality service and value. A smaller company can handle your issues, but can they act as business advisers, providing you with proactive advice?

I like your services, but they're not in our budget:

____ I'm glad to hear you like our products. Are funds available from other sources?
____ Proper allocation of funding is critical. How do you determine the disbursement?
____ What is it that you like, and how will it affect your budget?

How did you do? The answer to the first objection, about need, is the second choice. The correct response to the vendor objection is the third choice. The best response to the price objection is the third choice, and the final objection, about budget, is best answered by the second choice.

In view of the discussion we've already had, I would expect you to be able to pick out the proper responses easily. So let's raise the bar a bit and try an exercise that is more challenging and that requires you to focus on concepts. This is also a neutralizing exercise that requires you to give the correct response.

Determine the concepts of the following objections:

1. I'm concerned that your company can't meet our needs.

_____

2. We've had a bad experience with your company in the past.

_____

3. I'll review your literature.

_____

4. We don't have those concerns.

_____

5. You're always leaving your clothes on the floor.

_____

Let's see how you did in creating your own responses. These are my recommendations:

1. Providing the right solution is important.
2. Confidence in a company's ability is vital.
3. Making an informed decision is essential.
4. Identifying the areas in need of attention are critical to help a company grow.
5. Keeping the house neat is important (my wife will be thrilled to see that).

How did your concepts compare to mine? Now, on your own, try developing your own exercise from scratch. The goal is to create a list of issues that are of concern to your customer. Pick one of the most common objections that you listed in the earlier exercise, which could involve safety, compliance, or productivity. After selecting the objection, write a neutralizing statement (don't forget your agreement statement), and then write the companion question(s) you would use to overcome the objection. Try to identify a list of the issues of concern (e.g., "especially in areas of productivity"). This won't be easy, but it should get your creative juices going. If you just keep in mind the concepts and rules of neutralizing, you should be able to create very workable statements that are able to quash any objection.

Objection:

_____

_____

Step 1: Neutralizing

_____

_____

_____

Step 2: Question

_____

_____

_____

As I mentioned earlier, if you do a really terrific job on the first two neutralizing steps, you may not need to use the next steps, resolve the prospect's objection and check/proceed. If you've ever known a real skeptic, you might have had to prove to him that an outside temperature of thirty-two degrees is truly cold. So, for your own sake, it's a lot more productive for you to overcome the objections by neutralizing and asking questions based upon your funnels.

Resolve

Most customer objections fall into one of three basic categories—misconceptions, skepticism, and legitimate gripes. Misconceptions are common because many products and services are complex, but they're generally very simple to clear up. The skeptic remains unconvinced that your product or service will perform according to your claims or that your plan will solve his problems. He is simply being cautious and is looking for additional information. So it's up to you to allay his fears and prove that what you say will happen. Give solid evidence such as examples, testimonials, documented results, or the word of more senior personnel.

But what if the prospect has a legitimate objection? Maybe she has a valid point about some disadvantage in your product or service that doesn't meet her needs. Sometimes this does happen. Nothing's perfect. The objection can be about almost anything, but it most frequently concerns rates, terms, processing times, efficiency, or product capabilities. If that's the case, the only way to overcome these objections is to take the offensive—to point out the many advantages of your product and how they outweigh the disadvantages he has noted. Show her the big picture.

Let's see how well you can identify misconceptions, skepticism, and legitimate objections.

Please mark an M for misconception, an S for skepticism, and an L for legitimate.

1. ___ No budget, plus you don't offer discounts.
2. ___ I'm satisfied with my current vendor; we prefer that vendor's performance.
3. ___ Your prices are too high.
4. ___ We're concerned with environmental problems.
5. ___ We don't want to purchase now because we're experiencing a slowdown.
6. ___ I'm very comfortable with our current process.
7. ___ Every time I call, I can't get the information I need.
8. ___ Leave your literature, and I'll look it over.

     9. ____ Call me back next week.
   10. ____ Corporate mandates all of our decisions.

How did you do? I'll give you the answers, which may surprise you. First of all, there are no legitimate objections on the list. None. I marked Numbers 1, 3, 8, and 11 as misconceptions; and the rest reflect skepticism. If you didn't identify the misconceptions and skeptical statements the same way as I did, you're not necessarily wrong. Why? Because it really doesn't matter as long as they're not legitimate. I know that it's very difficult to distinguish between these two kinds of statements. But legitimate objections seem to pop right out at you. I know a salesperson who says she can feel them hitting her like a rock in her gut, because she knows they're true, and she has to really work to overcome them. Let me tell you a story that might really get to you but that also proves my point.

A family with a five-year-old boy just moved into a new neighborhood. This is a tough situation for any kid, getting to know the neighborhood and making new friends. Every day for weeks a group of kids would tease him, telling him, "We don't like you." Even though the little boy tried to ignore it, as his parents told him to, after weeks of this teasing, he came home in tears one day, crying to his mother, "Nobody likes me." His parents tried to reinforce the opposite, but he had heard the kids' taunting so often that he had begun to believe it.

This story is directly geared toward Mr. and Mrs. CSR. Every day you're going to hear a customer cite the objections that we have listed. And because you'll hear these objections every day, you may start to believe them. But in reality, 80 percent of all objections are misconceptions or skepticisms and are not legitimate at all. That means you can solve them. (P.S. The little boy eventually found his own group of friends who didn't taunt him, and they all lived happily ever after.)

Some Objections Can't Be Overcome

The point that is most important to keep with you is that you won't resolve all objections. Resolving two out of ten and clinching a sale is an excellent selling record. Neutralizing might net you four to five sales out of ten, but it's pretty remote—no matter if you beg—to resolve nine out of ten objections and make the sale. A batting average of more than .500 is truly amazing. Ask any baseball player. Of course, legitimate objections are the toughest to resolve, and there will be times that it proves impossible to resolve the objection.

If the objections are simple to overcome, it's easy to move ahead to presenting your solution. You can simply say something like, "Does that make sense to you?" The customer acknowledges that it does; then you can proceed to the next step in the quarter-half-quarter model. Like Monopoly's getting-out-of-jail rules, you must roll the right number before you can get out free. In this case you can't move forward until the objection is resolved; otherwise, you won't score a sale because these unresolved objections will still be hanging over your head. Bear in mind that as long as the CSR and the client are still talking, and the CSR is in control of the conversation, there's still a chance to make the sale. However, we all know at least one client who consistently throws objections at us and will probably never sign a contract. Some people just don't want to sign on the dotted line, no matter what.

Obviously, I can't guarantee these tactics will work every time. Still, they will probably help you eliminate half the objections you encounter, which leaves the other half, from customers who probably wouldn't buy the Louisiana Purchase at a bargain price. But, more often than not, these tactics will aid you in overcoming objections as long as you adhere to the consultative approach, because that will help to build a foundation and encourage long-term relationships with your clients. In doing so, there are several issues a CSR should consider.

First, it may take some time to change the customer's mind, and repeated attempts to get him to open up and give you a chance may be necessary. Oh, how I wish it weren't so, but, second, offering a great product or service that "everyone is using" doesn't mean this customer will see the value in it. Third, while you have earned the loyalty of certain clients over the years, so that you have the inside track on future sales, unfortunately, so have the companies you compete against. And, fourth, your product may go against the grain; some may even consider it newfangled. Perhaps employees will have to be trained to use it. Then there's the big cheese himself. Maybe your product requires that the president break a habit he's been comfortable with for years, one that has provided solid results. See what I mean about challenge?

As we discussed earlier in the book, change is difficult for people to accept. Computers, cellular phones, voicemail, electronic name/address organizers, fax machines—the list of modern products that people initially didn't see a real need for is endless. And they're all valid objections that some sorry salesperson heard dozens of times. I know that today I couldn't live without my computer or my cellular phone, but just a few years ago my attitude was, "Who needs it?" I still don't understand why the salesman who visited my office recently suggested that I create a Web site.

Looking at objections from this point of view zeroes in on why your role as a professional is to help the customer make the transition and see the advantages of trying something different. It's not that you're asking your customer to be a pioneer, but being the first can certainly have its advantages (multimedia laptop computer presentations, e-mail, paging). Still, the unknown can kill many deals. That's why you need to make the customer feel comfortable about focusing upon what is important to her and guide her to making the right decision. That's the essence of this four-step process.

Before we go on, I'm going to offer you a quick test that's designed to help you practice your responses to some common objections. There's a very good reason for this practice. What I want you to do is identify three of the most common objections you or your CSR receive, along with your response. It should only take you a few minutes.

To help you out, I'll give some examples that we've already discussed:

> "We're happy with our current vendor. Why should we change?"
> "Your company is so big, and we're just a small business."
> "I'm not sure we need that technology."

OK, now it's your turn.

Objection 1. _____
Response: _____

Objection 2. _____
Response: _____

Objection 3. _____
Response: _____

OK. Time is up. I'm guessing your lists include some of what my experience has shown to be the most common objections:

> "I'm satisfied with my current supplier."
> "I'm under contract until xxxxxx."
> "That decision gets handled in another office, department, or location or by another person."
> "We just completed our evaluation in that area and have just made a selection."
> "We have determined there is no need to change."
> "We had trouble with your company, product, or service in the past."
> "It seems you don't have the resources or availability that we are looking for."

Were you able to offset the objections by your responses and take control of the discussion? Armed with these common objections, you can plan ahead on how you're going to respond to these objections should they arise. This will give you a leg up on controlling the situation.

The Importance of Persistence

I've heard others say that objections are the stepping stones to closing the sale. Personally, I'd rather avoid the stones completely, because it would make my life a heck of a lot easier. But if you recall that New York Sales and Marketing Club survey referred to in Chapter 3, it suggested that 80 percent of all sales are made after the fifth objection. Remember, that's an average, so don't bother counting your customer's objections and figuring you only have two or three more to go before you get to the close.

The survey also points out that 80 percent of salespeople quit trying to sell the customer after the first objection (Customer: "We already have a vendor that we're happy with." CSR: "OK.") The survey concluded that 20 percent of the sales force often produces the majority of the sales. To put it into a non-mathematical format:

80 percent of the sales are made after the fifth objection

80 percent of salespeople quit after the first objection

20 percent of the sales force often produces the majority of sales

What does this survey tell you? You need to be persistent, even when confronting objections. And you need to realize that the customer might not acknowledge a need for change and might assert that he is satisfied, but there is enough of an indication that persistence along with a purpose (take back control of the situation!) will help you break through the roadblock and close more sales without turning around and heading home.

I'm sure most salespeople have stories about that one account that took months or even years to land. Sometimes that persistence translates into a rather unorthodox move. Let me tell you this story, compliments of my sales training friend at the international commodities *Fortune* 100 company. "Our CSRs used to simply say the customer is always right. Now it's a matter of finding out what the customer is trying to accomplish and what they need. You might say, 'Let me see if I can mix and match what's available.' Sometimes it may not be your own physical product that helps you put the deal together."

Let me sneak in here. This is another way of finding out the customer's needs, which may run beyond your particular product line, as well as identifying the reason for his resistance.

Sometimes you need to bend over backward to make the sale and to overcome the resistance. Now read on.

"We had a customer in Eastern Europe that needed financial assistance. It was a big customer, but they didn't have financially astute people to go to the bank [to secure the financing to buy the product/service]. We sent one of our financial people to go along with them, making it easier to do business, and we got the deal put together."

This is obviously an unusual sales situation, but I include it as an example of how creativity can help overcome the hurdles by eliminating the objection, luring the customer into a dialogue, and determining what the customer wants, and needs, to have done. In this case, the Eastern European company wanted to do business with my friend's company, but said, "Sorry, we can't pay for it." It was up to the salesperson to find out what was important to the customer and to explain his solutions clearly. Obviously, my friend's salespeople scored a touchdown with this issue. By asking questions and listening carefully, they determined that the customer's objections were based on a need for financing, and it was a simple matter of knowing what to ask for at the bank. Clearly, his approach worked just fine.

The Guiding Principles of Problem Resolution

Even though I've peppered this chapter with steps and processes designed to help you and your CSR overcome objections, I can simplify this for you by offering three guidelines that emphasize the primary points you need to remember. I call these the guiding principles. They are:

1. Maintain buyer focus.
2. Limit your initial comments.
3. Encourage customer dialogue.

1. *Maintain buyer focus.* It is essential to understand the customer's view of the objection or issue she is experiencing, questioning, or resisting. Because it's important to uncover this information if you're going to be able to proceed, I'd go so far as to say that it's critical that you or your CSRs ask dialogue

questions to glean the necessary information. In fact, that's why Step 2 of the four-step process introduced earlier in this chapter focuses on asking questions.

2. *Limit your initial comments.* This may be the toughest guideline to follow, especially if you're a talker, which covers most salespeople. Why? Because it's part of human nature to defend what we stand for. But you really need to limit your comments and focus on the customer, not on your viewpoint or rebuttal.

It seems that most of the time when a customer rattles off an objection, we feel compelled to explain, rationalize, or make the customer understand our thinking. Unfortunately, if we take this approach, we are losing touch with our customer's needs and replacing them with our need to justify our belief that the customer has it all wrong. Think about it. How many times has a customer said to you, "You don't have (the capacity, expertise, availability, track record)," and you've responded with some kind of answer or explanation. You defended your position. Too bad you didn't stop yourself and realize that this approach represents a break from consultative selling, where the focus is understanding the customer, in contrast to the traditional methods of selling where we present and close. You be the judge of what approach is best, and most productive.

3. *Encourage customer dialogue.* This point may sound repetitive; actually, it is, but it's so darned important. You and your CSRs are not going to get anywhere with the customer if you don't catch her in dialogue or a conversation. You need to lure the customer into continuous involvement and conversation about the issues and concepts surrounding the objections. Notice that I said "surrounding" the objection, not the specific objection. That's because that statement is the key to this entire model and approach to eliminating objections. Sustaining conversation improves your chances of stirring the customer's willingness to explore and express her opinions; consequently, it increases your chances of understanding the objections and discovering a satisfying response and solution.

Remember that little test about objections and responses I gave you a while back? Let's revisit those now and evaluate the responses you wrote down to your most common objections and see how they compare to the guiding principles of handling objections. As you assess your answers, I'm going to guess that you probably got some right, but you probably also violated at least one of the guiding principles, if not all of them. Keep in mind that some of the glitches in handling objections originate in our eagerness to explain to the customer that we have a great solution to their problems.

Remember, we talk too much. As I mentioned earlier, this eagerness probably stems from our belief in ourselves and in our product, which is not a bad attitude to have, but we really need to harness it for the right time and the right place.

Ready to move on? After you've dealt with the customer's objections, you are free to move ahead to the final step.

Check/Proceed

Basically, this fourth step is where you double-check the customer's responses and clarify where you stand. Frequently, one of the most puzzling wild card questions concerns price. With this issue, you're not just neutralizing; you're also negotiating, which can be a tricky process, so pay close attention. You can still neutralize objections that "the price is too high" by reminding the customer that he's getting the best value and saying, "Mind if I ask a few questions?" Don't be tempted to lower your price. A question for seasoned salespeople—how many times have you lowered your price and still not gotten the order or contract? By lowering the price, you're sending two fatal messages to the marketplace: (1) Your first price is not your best, and (2) your price can be lowered without a commitment from the customer.

When you say, "Can I ask you a few questions?," the customer is likely to say, "Sure, but make it quick." He figures you may be finished, but we know you're not. Do make it quick, because at this point the customer's coming from a position of strength and leverage, and you need to get it away from him so you can close the deal. Quickly, ask him these four questions:

1. Do you like our solution?
2. Do you feel we have the best solution?

3. Do you believe I have a complete understanding of your needs?
4. Do you feel my company has the resources to support you now and in the long term?

If you get yes answers to all these questions, then you've found out that you're the preferred choice, and you know your product is worth more money. What does this tell you? It says that, to the client, the price is not really too high, after all. That allows you to ask a fifth question: "It sounds like you have a preference dealing with us. We just have to figure out how to come to terms." That statement puts you in the driver's seat, putting you in control and transferring the leverage to you.

But what does it mean if you get a no to any of the four questions? Will you still get the order? Let's look at these questions again.

If the customer says no to the first question, you're in trouble. If it's the second, he's telling you that you didn't do a good job getting him to accept change and presenting your solution. A no answer to the third question means that you didn't do a good job in the "half" part of the quarter-half-quarter model, and a no to question 4 suggests that you didn't do a good job in the last quarter.

Negotiating Price

If you lower your price, you still will not get the order. And the customer will still occupy the position of strength and leverage. So what's the problem here? Well, maybe the customer still sees you and XYZ Company—your competitor—as the same.

On a brighter note, let's return to the yes answers, because I'm going to choose to be optimistic on your behalf (besides, after all the information I've given you in the previous chapters, all nos would make me look bad).

If you get yeses, you future her. Remember that concept? Because this objection concerns price, also remember that you're negotiating price, a factor that has to be resolved before you really reach agreement.

What price does she want? Expect her to be somewhat reasonable and ask for a reduction of 5 percent. Not that bad. So if you say to her, "If I go to my management and get the 5 percent discount, what would happen?" She'll probably say, "You'll get the order; then I'll have to think about it or take it to the board."

Now, let's evaluate what's happening here. The likelihood of her getting that 5 percent discount is remote because she's already indicated that you're the preferred vendor during that quick questioning sequence, right? So you call her back with a better price, but not exactly what she wanted, say, a 3 percent discount, would you still get the order? If the customer says yes, you know you're in a good position. If she says no, then you can still lower the price. But the odds are pretty good that the customer is not being totally truthful. What's more important, getting the contract or taking control of the situation from the customer and getting the price you want from her or not offering the price she wants to pay? I think you know the answer.

You now know how to identify objections and what they mean; realize they're not the end of the world; and know how to neutralize them in your favor. In Chapter 11 I discuss the raison d'être of this book—how to close your sale. I realize that, having made it through to this point, you may find it natural to simply mail the customer the contract. But you're not quite ready for that yet. You still have to gain the final commitment, and that's what the next chapter addresses. By the way, remember that sport utility vehicle I told you about earlier in this chapter? I bought it (it's a black Jeep Cherokee) from that pleasant salesperson, but not because she knew how to overcome my initial objection. I simply love that car!

11

"You Want to Give Greg and Mary Beth a Call?"

Gaining Commitment and Closing the Sale

Probably the most talked-about skill in selling is closing the sale. If you've ever had a chance to glance at books, magazines, and program brochures on selling, you've found hundreds of titles with the words "closing" or "closing the sale." In fact, if you look at my previous book, you'll find the word "closing" in the title. It's just one of those industry idioms, part of the jargon, like lawyers' practice of referring to their partners who bring in the most business as "rainmakers." I'm sure the customer service profession has its own jargon, too. In my case, and for other sales training materials, the reason is for the term simple. Bottom line—that jargon sells.

It doesn't take a great deal of gray matter to figure out why selling professionals are always looking for new ways to help them close a sale—money, and, in some cases, lots of it. You get paid or evaluated by how well you close the sale. Closing in many businesses has become the primary concern. How can you close the sale with the fewest calls? How can you close the sale and reduce the sales cycle? How can you close the sale before the end of the month, quarter, or year to hit your predetermined numbers? And, for many of you who never really close the sale, how can you influence the customer well enough so that, when the opportunity to buy your product or service arises, the customer will think of you and recommend, purchase, or request what you have to offer?

Closing the sale has always been viewed as the pinnacle—the measurement of success for salespeople. Your associates ask you, "Did you or didn't you close the sale?" and give you "that look" if you say something like "Not yet, but it should be soon." And they're thinking to themselves, "Yeah, right." Those who do close the sale reap great rewards, including respect from their peers and superiors and maybe hearty congratulations from their associates, depending on the nature of the sale (maybe they closed a big contract with a company that no one else has been able to get to first base with). Those who don't close a sale often struggle with doubt and frustration, to say nothing of the looks of pity or disdain that they may get from their associates.

In this chapter we explore closing the sale, but from a different perspective. It's not the pinnacle you've always viewed it as, but just another part in the complicated puzzle of the sales process that is completed when the customer buys your product or service. Even though, historically, the closing has typically been viewed as the endgame, the crowning moment, the handshake, I believe it's just as important to examine the factors that lead up to this moment. In fact, I believe it's even more important to look at those elements. I'm talking about determining the benchmark for the ideal set of practices designed to build relationships, seek agreement and commitment that lead to change, and win the eventual purchase, recommendation, or ordering of the products or services you represent.

From this perspective, successfully completing each of these parts constitutes "closing the sale," because if you don't, for example, get a commitment to change from the customer, you have missed an important element of the sales process, one that can have a major effect on the end result.

You may think of this chapter as a summary of the elements you learned in the previous chapters, and, in some ways, it is. But it goes a step further. As you proceed through this chapter, keep in mind that the major steps I describe are all connected and build on each other. You know how small children, playing with their building blocks, put one on top of the other? Each block depends on the other, although the single blocks alone do not build a sturdy tower. The child is likely to build the tower too high, so it eventually topples over, or she may just knock it over and think it's great fun.

Each sales segment is also a building block, but you want to avoid building a tower that could topple over, so you reinforce it by putting more than one block on each level. When each level is completed, you put on the next one. Keep this building-block scenario in mind while I help you determine the best way to proceed through the sales process, using all the components in the most efficient manner to eventually close the sale (or build a study tower) by closing each step of the sales process in order.

For example, we're going to look at the tried and true notion of buying signals and determine what their place and function is for closing a sale. However, because this sales truism as an accurate read on buying signals alone isn't sufficient, it's also critical to look at what it really takes to advance the selling process to the close. Remember, it takes not just one element but all of them together, working together in an organized manner, to reach your goals. If you excel in one area but fall down in another, you run the risk of having the whole deal falling apart. That's why you need to review the critical areas as a whole—action steps, key occurrences, the sales cycle, and the creation of a sales strategy that identifies the buying influencers.

Counting Your Fs, or the Art of Reading Signals Accurately

Let's begin with one of my favorite activities—an exercise. It's really a game I call "Count the Fs." I want you to read the following sentence, count the Fs, and write down how many you find. Obviously, this is a pretty simple exercise, one that any five-year-old could do. And if I were to ask you if you really believe you can accomplish this correctly, of course you'd say yes. So let's do it.

"Feature films are the result of years of scientific study combined with the experience of years."

How many did you find? Three? Four? Five? Six? The correct answer is that there are 6 Fs in that sentence—"feature," "films," "scientific," and the three "ofs." Missed those, huh? In my seminars, I ask the participants to complete the same game. Would you believe that at least half the people miss the "ofs?" There's a good reason for this. When you read the word "of," the "f" sounds like a "v," so you don't pick up the word. However, those of you who got four or five Fs, well, I'm a bit concerned about you. Perhaps you need to get your eyes and ears checked.

Why bother with this simplistic exercise? Well, I'm certain that if I had bet you a dollar that you couldn't count all of the Fs, many of you would have taken me up on it. A dollar may not be a lot of money, and, besides, how hard could this be? Of course you could accurately count all of the Fs. But what really happened? Remember, something like half of the people got this so-called simplistic exercise wrong.

OK, I can hear you now. How does this relate to sales? I'll tell you how. Think about buying signals, which we define as verbal or physical signs that indicate the customer's initial interest in your product or service. They typically occur during the building relationship part of the sales cycle. What happens if you misinterpret a customer's verbal or physical action as reflecting true interest on his part when, in fact, he's got a cold and is just clearing his throat? To yourself, you're saying, "Wow, this guy is really interested. I bet I can close this sale in only three steps." But remember, buying signals are just one piece of the selling pie, so how much weight do they really carry by themselves? Not much. But they do lead you on to the next step. Later, we'll return to buying signals to examine how they can help you.

Consider this example for the seasoned salespeople, or for the CSRs who have a specific goal to attain. Let's say your manager asks you, "How is it going with the EZY account?" You respond, "Just great. It should close any week now." A couple of weeks go by, and your manager asks again, "How is it going at the EZY account?" And you respond, "Just great. It should close any day now." A few more days go by, and your manager asks again, "How's it going with the EZY account?" and you say, "I should close any hour now!"

Do you get the picture? How long can this go on? In sales, we tend to be that confident with many customers, believing everything is on track, when in reality some pieces are missing; as in that simplistic game, maybe we aren't counting all of the F's. Is it possible that you moved the sales process along too quickly or didn't confirm your position by checking your progress? You betcha. To handle this problem, you need to learn how to build a road map—what I call a critical path—to closing, whether or not you actually close the sale. That's why you need to focus on the methods that help you measure your progress and effectively determine where you stand in the sales cycle.

Key Occurrences

A major element of building the critical path to closing is what I call key occurrences. You must gain acceptance, an agreement, or a commitment from your customer on these topics or elements so that you can track the progression of the relationship and the sales process. To explain this aspect of the process, I have to tell you a great story that I swear is true. I call it the Greg and Mary Beth story. It may not be Hemingway, but I think you'll enjoy it. Read on.

The Saga of Greg and Mary Beth

Several years ago on one Saturday afternoon, six couples, including my wife, Annette, and myself, got together to enjoy the afternoon followed by dinner. It just so happened that our afternoon plans were shorter than we had planned, so we had some time to spare before dinner. So the six couples—the five married ones and the unmarried couple, Greg and Mary Beth, whom all of us knew from our college days—decided to grab a drink before dinner. As we started to laugh about college stories, one of the men of our group turned to Greg and Mary Beth and less than tactfully asked, "You know, we've known each other since college, and that's a long time. And during that time the two of you have been dating. When do you think the both of you are going to take the plunge and finally get married?"

Needless to say, Greg and Mary Beth were very surprised by the question, and probably a bit embarrassed, too, because right after dinner Mary Beth said she didn't feel well, and the two of them left before dessert.

All of us felt bad, but the fellow in our group who had asked the initial question turned to us and asked, "Well, now that they are gone, what do you think? Will they get married or not?" As an aside to this story, by now you know my frame of reference is very narrow, so if you've read the book this far you know I see everything in terms of a sales cycle. Back to the story. So I said, "You have to figure out if the occurrences are there." Now, fortunately I wasn't narrow-minded enough to say key occurrences, but you get the idea. Everyone at the table asked me, "What do you mean?" As if I were at a seminar, I proceeded to explain.

"It's simple," I told them. "Occurrences are indications that the relationship is maturing, advancing." Someone in the group asked, "Such as what? Give us an example. How can you measure that?" So I continued my "lesson." I told them it was simple, but only if you notice the little things, such as, for example, whether Greg buys Mary Beth a nice gift, such as an expensive camera, a CD player, or a piece of art that he knows, if they get married, he'll ultimately get back. It's kind of like a gift on loan.

Everyone else asked what could we add to this list. At this point it became a game. We came up with a variety of items— Greg and Mary Beth might spend more time with the potential in-laws, possibly getting together at some event like a fundraiser; they might sponsor a niece or nephew in a religious function or sporting event. Toward the bottom of the list, we put the engagement, rehearsal dinner, and wedding.

All of this was written on a piece of paper. The next day, Sunday, I went into my office and wrote this list on my computer and sent out copies to all of the couples who were with us that night, except for Greg and Mary Beth, of course. What happened next was really bizarre. Over a period of the next several months, many of us took advantage of any opportunity to spend time with Greg and Mary Beth. We would call them or vice versa and make plans, say, to go to dinner. Often they would say, "We'll meet you at the restaurant," but the person talking to them would jump in and say, "Oh no, we'll pick you up." Sure, it was sneaky, but when we picked her up, we would go into Mary Beth's townhouse and look around to notice if there was anything new. The anointed sneak might say, "Hey, this artwork looks new. It's really interesting. When did you get it?" And, of course, Mary Beth would say, "Thank you. Greg got it for me." Snicker, snicker. So the next day we'd call our friends and say, "Cross it off the list."

You can probably figure where this story is heading. Needless to say, today Greg and Mary Beth are married and recently had twins. But what was really interesting—and funny, too, for sure—is that from the day we started the list until the day they were married, we ended up crossing off everything on that list! And, yes, Greg and Mary Beth are very happy, thank you.

Your Client Has a List, Too

The point of my version of a soap opera is that your customer, too, has a list, which indicates the relationship is progressing. It may not include a CD player or artwork, but you do need to identify the list, develop the cycle, and move toward gaining commitment on all of the items on the list. To determine your particular cycle, or critical path, first you need to figure out which occurrences take place in your most successful sales scenarios, or, in the case of CSRs who have yet to make a sale, in your most successful fabricated scenario. Identifying these elements and setting them as a benchmark for your critical path will enable you to measure and focus your sales progression. In other words, your critical path will be based on the elements that have worked the best for you in the past.

By using this process, you'll be able to close effectively by identifying and clarifying the customer's statements and assessing his willingness to proceed, while also pinpointing your critical path for closing the sale. When you determine the specific path of action and commitments for your customer, you can recognize, categorize, and clarify his buying signals as well as push the process forward. Remember, closing is not an event that happens at the end of the sales process. As we've been discussing, I choose to define it as a series of activities that occur throughout the entire sales cycle. Unfortunately, if you were to ask the majority of salespeople their definition of closing, the most popular answer would probably be "getting the order." That may be fine for them, but it's not OK with me, and it shouldn't be OK with you, either. Yes, that's how salespeople get paid. But—here's my blasphemy—closing is not just getting the sale. It's something more. It's gaining commitment to your sales call's primary objectives, as well as an acceptance and agreement to your key occurrences. If this pattern is followed, then getting the order is just another criterion on a long list of things that have to occur to close the sale. Remember my Greg and Mary Beth story? Spending time with the in-laws was just another item on the list that led to the marriage. (Come to think of it, meeting the in-laws could change some people's minds. . . .)

I like this approach, not just because I created it, but because looking at closing from this point of view takes the pressure off the "big close" and spreads it out more evenly over the entire process, so the final questions take on the same importance as all of the other commitment statements that occur during the cycle. That's kind of refreshing, isn't it? To most people, sales are all about pressure. That's probably why many CSRs didn't choose the profession to begin with. In fact, I have a friend who would probably be very good at sales—she's believable and passionate about what she happens to be talking about, and she is a former reporter, to boot, so she knows how to ask questions and listen. But when she is asked why she doesn't go into sales, her answer is always the same—"I couldn't take the pressure, or the rejection." But with my approach, the pressure is relieved, and so is the feeling of rejection.

As with any destination, you need to know where you are going in sales in order to map out the places along the way that will get you there. That's why at this point you need to create your sales cycle for the specific business scenario, determine and implement your customer action steps and key occurrences, and understand the decision-making process of an organization.

This process also includes identifying key influencers and the company's organizational issues.

The Sales Cycle

By definition, a sales cycle is an estimated or projected number of steps required to develop a customer and to win a commitment to action—the first step in closing. The cycle sets your steps in a logical progression. Remember that New York Sales and Marketing Club survey from Chapter 3? It also revealed information on sales cycles. According to the survey, 81 percent of the time sales are closed on the fifth step of the cycle. The survey suggested that the first step in every cycle start with "Initiate the Relationship" and that the cycle conclude with the "Step to Close." What comes in between?

Depending on your situation, it's the number of steps you need to build a relationship, seek a commitment to change, present a solution, seek customer involvement and support, and finally close the sale. Other steps could be on-site visits, demonstrations, meeting with additional decision makers, product or services presentations, and evaluations. Remember, each step is considered a major event or occurrence, or, to turn it around, a major event or occurrence is one step in the entire scheme. A typical sales cycle is one, three, or five steps, depending on what you're selling and who the customer is.

For argument's sake, let's say this cycle is yours—build a relationship, seek a commitment to change, present a solution, seek customer involvement and support, close the sale. The cycle will never change, but the number of phone calls you make to get the job done can and will change, meaning that each sales call is not considered a step in the cycle, but several phone calls that allow you to succeed at, say, getting your customer's involvement and support is a cycle step. Also remember that "initiate the relationship" is always the first step, and "closing the sale" is always the final step.

Now, it's time for you to develop your own industry-specific sales cycle. Don't be afraid to give this some thought before jumping in.

_____

_____

_____

_____

_____

_____

All done? Look at it again, and make sure it's in a sequential order; also check the flow of the cycle. That same kind of orderly progression governs your sales cycle when you are designing it.

Designing a Logical, Sequential Sales Cycle

Let's take an additional "big picture" look at selling itself. This shouldn't surprise you, but because selling is about developing strong relationships, analogies about developing personal relationships can spill into the explanation of our process. Just as in any relationship that you want to last a long time, for the most part you don't want to rush into a sales relationship; on the other hand, you don't want to take it too slow. For example, let's look at dating. I'm guessing most of you are familiar with this topic, so I believe it can work as a good analogy to validate the sales cycle you just designed. Before I give you this analogy, I wish to offer a caveat. The dating sequence is based upon something Generation X-ers might not be able to relate to at all. And I guess I'm showing my age, because this is how we dated when I was in college. So, read it for the analogy, and not as some kind of historical literature. Here goes.

When you meet a person for the first time and mutually decide to see each other on a date (I'm assuming, of course, that it's still called that), a popular first date in our society is to meet for lunch. Now, lunch has a lot of advantages—it's short, so if it isn't going well you always have an excuse to leave. Especially if it's during the workweek, you can arrive separately, so you don't have to rely on each other for transportation, and you can come and go as you please. Also, a restaurant is a public place, so there is safety in being out in the open, and the check is probably affordable for whomever is paying (or if you're both picking up your own tabs).

So Step 1 in the dating cycle is lunch. Let's say the lunch goes well and you discover you have things in common, so probably the next step is to try to spend more time with each other, something like dinner and a movie. The next step, Step 2, is dinner (or sharing pizza). Dinner gives you an opportunity to get to know each other a little better, and the movie gives you a chance to spend more time together, but it takes the pressure off of having to talk for another hour or so because you're watching the movie. And, after the movie, it gives you something to talk about over a cup of coffee or a drink.

If that evening goes well, then the third step in your dating cycle might be spending an afternoon together (Step 3). That could mean going to a museum, ballgame, zoo, beach, or whatever. In this step the time commitment is increased rather dramatically, because this step will probably take up a good bit of the afternoon and perhaps last into the evening. During this step, friends may also be introduced.

Step 4 is where the relationship is likely to take a giant leap forward. This is the step where you might meet family members by attending a family function or plan a short weekend getaway (perhaps a ski trip). Once you reach Step 5, things are pretty well on their way, and I'll leave what happens here up to your imagination (just remember that I'm waiting until Step 5 for your imagination to go into overdrive).

By now you're probably getting the picture. Let's review the logical process you went through: Step 1 is lunch; Step 2 is dinner; Step 3 is an afternoon or a day together, possibly with friends; Step 4 is an introduction to family members or a quick weekend getaway; and I'm guessing that at Step 5 some closing took place.

Selling is much the same thing, a process of steps to the close. If the process is pushed forward too quickly, failure is probable. For example, if you jump from Step 1 (lunch) to Step

4 or 5, I think you'll agree the process will break down because you are moving too fast. The same is true in selling; if you don't map out the process and instead move too fast, the process will break down. But the opposite could be just as damaging; if you wait too long, other players may get into the picture, the interest level may wane, and you might not have the chance to close the sale.

The point I'm trying to make here is that determining your sales cycle and checking its logical progression is important to developing strong business relationships. You can't expect to move from Step 1 to Step 4 or 5, just as you can't complete Step 1 and never follow up and expect to get the sale. The first part of that sentence is just as illogical as the second part. As I've said many times, the sales cycle gives you the road map to success. Once you figure out your cycle, it shouldn't change. Only the number of sales calls, or phone calls, that it takes to execute the steps can change. For example, if in Step 1 you try to move to meet, or speak with, additional buying decision makers and your current contact puts up a roadblock, you know it will take more calls to move through the process. On the other hand, if during your first meeting or phone call your customer says (remember, he may now be a buddy because you've been solving his problems for a long time as his CSR), "Can I introduce you to others involved in this project?" you know the cycle is progressing faster than expected. The sales cycle is a method of measurement in developing a customer, in a profession that isn't prone to measurements, so, if talking to additional buying decision makers is your Step 2, you know that once you complete this step, you can move on to Step 3. In other words, determining and checking your cycle keeps you on track and enables you to know exactly where you are and where you have to go.

Now, please take a minute and review the logical progression of the sales cycle that you wrote a little earlier in this chapter. As you review your cycle, use these steps as a benchmark that you can compare your cycle with:

Step 1. Initiate relationships.
Step 2. Continued discovery with additional decision makers.

Step 3. Presenting solutions.
Step 4. Product/service demonstration.
Step 5. Proposal/close.

Primary, Secondary, and Minimum Objectives

Now that you have identified your sales cycle, you have completed one of the biggest steps in closing the sale. By figuring out your cycle, you have also figured out your closes. Let me explain further. Now that you know your cycle, you also know what you will be closing on, because every step of your cycle has a primary, secondary, and minimum objective. Here are definitions of these levels of objective:

- Your cycle's *primary* objective is acceptance to move on to the next step in the cycle.
- Your cycle's *secondary* objective is commitment to or acknowledgment of a key occurrence.
- Your cycle's *minimum* objective is the execution of the step's title.

When opening up your call in the first quarter of the quarter-half-quarter model, you state the goal or objective. The goal of the sales call is your cycle's *primary* objective, which is always the next step in your cycle. For example, if you were to use the cycle I listed earlier, the goal or close for Step 1, initiate the relationship, is to get to Step 2, meeting with additional decision makers. Therefore, in your opening comments describing what you want to accomplish, you would mention your intention of coming back to meet with others (or having a second phone call be a conference call with others) to continue the information-gathering and discovery process. By identifying what you want to accomplish at the beginning of the call, you have told the customer your goal and have indicated the direction of the call. Identifying your goals or knowing where you want to go makes it much easier for you to close this step.

This same principle holds true in the dating cycle I discussed earlier. I'm sure that if the lunch is going well, somewhere in the conversation, the idea of going out to dinner and a movie might be mentioned. But you don't want to drop hints that won't be accepted or that could be ignored, so you have to come up with the next concept of closing—the secondary objective. This objective tests the waters and builds a foundation of success for your primary objective. Secondary objectives identify the key occurrences in the sales cycle; key occurrences determine the progression of the cycle and identify milestones, markets, or issues that indicate a customer's willingness (or that of another party) to move forward in the relationship.

Remember the Greg and Mary Beth story? Here's how you use the ideas that were played out in that story. In every sales cycle, you need to identify a key occurrence. This occurrence provides you with information and a method to check the cycle's progress, giving you the green light to move to the primary objective (or the yellow, to be more cautious). During every step in the cycle you should have at least one key occurrence. Just as the cycle has a natural or logical progression, so do key occurrences. For example, if Step 1 is to initiate a relationship with a decision maker and Step 2 is to get your original contact to introduce you to others, a key occurrence in the first step would be to seek the original contact's acceptance to change or act as your coach or advocate. You should know if this first contact will be your coach before you ask to move to Step 2. By securing a commitment to a key occurrence, you are increasing the likelihood that you will reach your primary objective.

To help you in the process of applying and understanding key occurrences or *secondary* objectives, I'm going to give you a small exercise on key occurrences. Please take a minute and complete this exercise by identifying what you think are key occurrences to measure the progression of the sales process:

Key occurrences: An indication of milestone, markers, or issues that indicate a willingness from the prospect to move forward in the relationship.

Examples: Customer tours your location.

Customer is willing to look at alternatives or change.

Customer agrees to your benefits/solutions.

Customer agrees to be your champion/coach.

Customer introduces you to key decision makers.

Identify which of the following are key occurrences:

____ 1. Requests your literature
____ 2. Agrees to arrange an appointment with additional key personnel
____ 3. Asks you to call back in a week
____ 4. Expresses a willingness to change
____ 5. Sees your product/service as a solution
____ 6. Agrees to be your coach/champion
____ 7. Wants you to review applications and give suggestions
____ 8. Leans forward and expresses interest (for face-to-face meetings only)
____ 9. Expresses serious interest and vows not to waste your time
____10. Thanks you for a great presentation and your efforts

That didn't take long, did it? The answer: items 2, 4, 5, and 6 are key occurrences. The items identified in this exercise are only a few of the key occurrences you can come up with. However, this list contains some very important key occurrences that I recommend you integrate into your sales cycles.

The last objective of your cycle is the *minimum* objective. Minimum objectives are defined as simply the execution of the step's title or the very least you want to accomplish. For example, if you are in Step 4 or 5, presenting a proposal or providing a demonstration of your product, the minimum objective is simply to explain the proposal or conduct the demonstration. (P.S. to CSRs: Even though the assumption is that you will be selling over the phone, depending on your product, you may need to invite the prospect to the company for the demonstration, especially if the product is too complicated to adequately describe over the phone. You'll have to work this out with your supervisor or sales management.)

The combination of the three objectives—primary, secondary, and minimum—integrated into your sales cycle builds you a perfect critical path. It identifies the major elements you need to gain acceptance and agreement to move the process forward.

I would like you to design your own critical path/sales cycle. This is an important learning tool for you, so please take several minutes to figure out the appropriate secondary objectives for your cycle when writing your primary and minimum objectives. The primary and the minimum objectives should be simple to determine, because the primary is always the next step in the cycle and the minimum is just the execution of the step's title.

OK? Now that you've completed the design of your sales cycle, the last piece of your plan before you develop your strategy is to include action steps in each step of the cycle.

Action Steps

I define action steps as those steps that qualify the customer's intent and interest in your product or service. Action steps retrieve buy-in and mutual collaboration from the customer. The customer offers an action using his own time and resources toward the completion of your objective of the development of the relationship. In simpler terms, the customer does something for you in exchange for your doing something for him. Common action steps are asking the customer to complete a questionnaire, attend a meeting hosted or sponsored by your company, or introduce you to additional key decision makers. In the whole scheme of things, I think this is a pretty simple concept to understand—I give you something and you give me something back in return.

Let's try to complete that sales cycle you've been working on. Select an appropriate action step for each step in your cycle. By doing this, you have increased the participation level of your customer as well as provided yet another indicator to measure your progress.

All done? I believe congratulations are in order. You've just completed your sales cycle. Completing this step marks a major accomplishment in knowing how and when to close. By completing your cycle, you have just identified your sales path, and you now have a road map to developing a relationship that leads to business. Following and using this path provides you with the benchmarks for sales success in your marketplace.

Does that sound good? Think you're finished because I've congratulated you? Uh-uh. Now that your cycle is completed, you have accomplished the first step in closing—commitment to action. By following your sales cycle, you now know what commitment to action you will be asking for. Therefore, whether scheduling an appointment on the phone or conducting a sales call, you should know exactly what step of the cycle you are in and what your next commitment or close is.

Every time you open your sales call, you should give an indication of the goal of the call, which, in turn, is the same as the call's primary objective. That states the next step in your sales cycle. Let me say that one more time, with a bit more emphasis, perhaps: When you open up the sales call, you should state the goal of the call. The goal that you give is the same thing you will be seeking a commitment toward at the end of the sales call. And that's the primary objective of the specific sales cycle you are in, which is also the title of the next step in your cycle. This is a very important concept to remember. By stating your primary objective in your opener, you are giving your customer a preview of where you want your sales call to go. When you are wrapping up your sales call, your closing comments will be framed around gaining commitment to your primary objective for the call.

Remember the dating analogy that I gave you so that we could finalize this step? You may remember that I said it is always good to send out a trial balloon during the date so that you can increase the likelihood of gaining acceptance of your primary motives. The checking mechanism that I suggested was to ask for a secondary or key occurrence during your date as a way of seeing if everything is going well.

Using that same analogy or checking mechanism, during the sales call you need to check how well you are doing in the call by sending out a trial balloon to seek acceptance or a commitment to a key occurrence and an action step. I don't mean anything like, "So, how am I doing?" If you receive positive feedback in these two areas, that is a signal to move forward to requesting a commitment to your call's primary objective. By checking the progress of your call with your secondary objectives and seeking commitment to your primary objective, you can smoothly move through your sales cycle.

When you gain acceptance to more than fifteen different closes, that's five steps with three objectives each. And, if I might say, that's pretty darn good. The last objective, the grand old "getting the order," is simply just another step in the cycle. Looking at it this way, it's no big deal, because this approach takes the emphasis from the close and focuses it on the entire process. If you didn't get this point completely before, I'm certain you understand the ramifications of it now. If you adopt my recommendations, gaining acceptance to change or arranging a meeting with additional decision makers carries the same weight as the close and enables you to easily proceed and measure your progress from one cycle to the next.

Buying Signals

The second step in closing is recognizing, categorizing, and clarifying buying signals. Buying signals are verbal and physical signs that show the customer's initial interest in your product/service or solution. Physical and verbal cues don't always have any significant meaning in terms of your accomplishing your final close, so be careful not to jump the gun on these. A buying signal can be a sign that the customer is starting to realize his acceptance of your ideas and solutions, but a buying signal is not necessarily a sign that the customer is ready to write you a check. Instead look at buying signals as opportunities for you to understand the customer's interest level, an avenue for you to explore what the customer is really saying and understand the actual intent of his comments or actions.

Think about this. Would you agree that just because someone leans toward you, that doesn't indicate she will place an order with you? What a buying signal can do for you is provide a forum to qualify the customer and her statements. When addressing a customer's response with reference to a buying signal, it is important to do three things to maximize the possibility of a positive outcome and avoid a false interpretation of his comments or actions:

1. Recognize buying signals.
2. Accurately categorize.
3. Clarify the intent.

They are *recognize, categorize,* and *clarify.* Even through the third level—clarify—is where you're going to be spending most of your time during this process, I'll begin with the logical order, first explaining the first level—*recognition.* This step is quite simple. It involves identifying whether the buying signals are verbal or physical. The problem at times is that we tend to get carried away. The signals are viewed as a sign from above, and we move too quickly. On the other hand, the second level—*categorization*—helps prevent us from selling prematurely and provides us with a real read on the comments and conditions.

Maybe I shouldn't be telling you this because then I'd be revealing my book test secrets, but I'll tell you anyway. If you were to string all or many of the comments written down in that exercise together, it would probably be fair to say that the customer was positive. And if you did start to hear all of these comments at once, my advice would be to close quickly. But let's face it: How often do you really close quickly in the real world? Remember, the focus of this chapter is that there is a series of cycles and steps you need to go through to make the sale happen.

The final point of analyzing buying signals is *clarification.* The easiest way of doing this is to acknowledge the customer's comments and use the futuring technique on the customer to understand what his comments and actions really mean. All too often we take the customer's statements at face value and don't explore and probe them the way we should.

Let me give you a more complete definition: Qualify the customer's buying signal by questioning the intent or insinuation of his statement or action. This enables you to confirm the category of the buying signal as well as receive a clear definition from the customer about the true meaning or indication of his motive/action. By clarifying, you can support the good feeling that the customer is having about your product/service or uncover doubt and determine his actual interest level.

For years you have been conditioned to acknowledge buying signals, ranging from the customer's nodding his head to comments like, "This sounds good. What's your availability?" or "We sure could use your service to help resolve our problems." For the most part, comments like these and hundreds of others that you may have heard in the past have been viewed as positive—a comment in the right direction. Earlier in the book, I discussed how a large majority of a customer's comments aren't as positive as we would like them to be. (Remember the positive, negative, and noncommittal? Those are the three categories to look for as you evaluate the buying signals. More about that shortly.)

Because you as a CSR experience challenges on a daily basis, and moving into the inside sales role will present even more challenges in your pursuit to build relationships and close more business, you should know that, at times, salespeople have latched onto traditional or classic buying signals that customers send out without verifying their actual level of interest. I remember several years ago attending a seminar by a psychologist turned sales trainer who stressed identifying buying signals as important elements of closing a sale. As part of the seminar, we had to role-play different movements and comments so that we could identify the customer's moves and comments to our advantage. I, along with probably hundreds of other salespeople, thought this was great until I began to realize that it didn't really work. The trainer had thrown in, for example, the idea that we should look around the exec's office and comment on the items he had there, such as family pictures and awards, as a means of building rapport. I must have complimented more execs on their ugly children than you can count. Listen carefully, she told us. Watch the exec's movements. But that Sunday morning TV commercial keeps replaying in my mind—"That was then. This is now."

In reality, many buying signals that you hear today really don't lead to immediate sales. Buying signals are simply a way for the customer to learn more about you or disqualify you. That is quite a contrast, isn't it? Are the comments the customers makes indicative of interest, or are they masking their feelings and trying to control the sales call to get the information they want from you?

I'm don't really put a lot of credence in buying signals. Bet you couldn't tell, right? With all the parity in today's marketplace, combined with the pressure placed on the customer to make the right choice, a buying signal is not what it takes in today's business world to bring the process to a favorable close. However, I do believe it's important for CSRs to learn what the signals are, what to listen for, and how to interpret them. Otherwise, they can really throw you for a loop and affect your success. Remember, as we've been discussing throughout this chapter, closing is an action that happens with each individual step in your sales cycle. A buying signal won't necessarily affect that closing one way or another.

When sorting buying signals, there are three categories you have to be concerned with. Remember these?

- Negative—displays negative, uninterested attitude toward your product or service
- Noncommittal—an impartial attitude toward your thoughts and ideas
- Positive—displays a supportive, optimistic position where an intent of action is present

I'm guessing you'll remember these terms from earlier in the book, where you did an exercise on them (see Chapter 4). What's important, though, is when assessing any customer statement there must be an intent to action for it to be considered positive. In fact, any single customer statement (or buying signal), if taken out of context, could fall under the category of noncommittal. Before you disagree with me, ask yourself, could the customer make these same statements to my competition? Do these statements really indicate the customer's willingness to move forward? Is the customer masking and not revealing his true feelings? Taking a more cautious approach lets you clarify the statement position, allows you to move forward without going too far and damaging the customer or account.

Here are a few examples. If the customer says, "Based on what you have said, I would like to receive a proposal from you," your response should be, "I'd be glad to. What do you want the proposal to accomplish for you, and, after you receive it, what do your believe will happen?"

If the customer says, "I've narrowed the list down to you and the XYZ Company. Please review your proposal and resubmit your final offer," you should respond, "I'm glad we are a finalist. What are the criteria you are now looking at, and what happens if we meet them?"

Get the idea? You're making sure you understand exactly what the customer is saying and what he wants from you so that you don't run around like a chicken with his head cut off trying to please the client by completing A when he's really looking for B. Compare this with a remark my former journalist friend once mentioned to me as her secret for keeping her editor happy. When her editor gives her a story assignment, she asks him many questions about what kind of story he's looking for and what he expects her to find during the course of her interviews. Once she writes the story and hands it in, as is usually the case, the editor makes some comments and asks her to rework some of the story. Her theory is that people tend to know what they don't want but don't really know what they do want until they actually see it. So she questions him carefully about what he's looking for in order to clarify his comments and questions. She calls this action "giving the editor what he wants" to keep him happy.

In that same vein, by clarifying what the customer is saying, you end up giving the customer what he wants, enabling you to close that step and move on to the next.

Customer Service

It might seem odd to you that I would end this chapter with some comments on customer service. After all, the point of this entire book has been how to convert customer service representatives into an inside sales team. But just because CSRs move into sales doesn't mean that all-important customer service should fall by the wayside. Let's say you do end up making a sale to the Harvey Smith Company. You still have to service the client by making sure he gets his order when it's promised and that there are no problems with it; check in with him periodically to make sure everything is running smoothly, perhaps offer to take him out to lunch, and basically try to keep him as a happy camper. Remember, the contract is not a lifetime agreement. It will come up for renewal, probably after a year. And it would be a heck of a lot simpler to have the customer sign a renewal contract than to have to convince him again that your solution is the best for his company.

Think about your own personal experiences. If you buy a car at Go-Go Car Auto Dealer, when you take the car in for repairs, you'll certainly want to do business with that dealer again if he offers you a loaner car while he works on your car. (I confess, this is a top-of-mind topic with me. Remember my beautiful Jeep that I loved? It had a problem, I took it in for repairs, and the dealer not only argued with me about who should pay for it but also refused to give me a loaner car while he kept it for repairs. Needless to say, I'm not so sure I'd do business with that dealer again.)

In contrast, have you ever purchased an expensive item of clothing that ripped or was damaged the first time you wore it? You took it back to the retailer and found the store so difficult to deal with, even when you asked to speak to the manager, that you just tossed down the item and walked out of the store? Bad customer service. Remember my new office phone system? Something isn't working right with it, and I'll find out this week how good the vendor's promised customer service is. I'm choosing to be optimistic.

Notice that in almost every instance (except for my Jeep, of course, and the clothes retailer), the salesperson had to close the sale the first time but understood the importance of good customer service. I'm assuming that you do, too, because closing a sale does not end when the customer signs on the bottom line.

Speaking of closing, because this ties up the final instructional chapter of this book, I bet you'll be looking for a heading or chapter entitled "Closing the Sale." Well, quit looking, because you're not going to see one, and here's why. For starters, I've already explained it. No, you're not missing a chapter, but perhaps you're missing the point. As the bulk of this chapter explains, you're closing the sale every time you close a step of your selling cycle, so you alleviate the pressure on a "final step." You closed the sale when you completed Step 1, initiated relationships; Step 2, continued discovery with additional decision makers; Step 3, presented solutions; Step 4, demonstrated your product/service; Step 5, presented proposal/closed—if this was your chosen sales cycle.

Congratulations. I officially anoint you an advanced customer service representative.

Conclusion

"The Party's Over; It's Time to Call It a Day"

Final Thoughts and Advice

You know that classic riddle, "How do you get to Carnegie Hall? Practice, practice, practice." That's probably the best kind of advice I can give you at this point. But I'd like to reiterate some final points and reminders to help you succeed in your journey from the role of customer service representative to advanced customer service representative:

1. *Recognize the change to an ACSR.* This will be difficult at first. Change is difficult for everybody. Remember, it's a mind-set.
2. *Manage your management.* You'll need to adapt to their culture, and they to yours. It will probably be a struggle at first due to that "red light" syndrome, but you'd be surprised how well people respond to positive suggestions that can affect the bottom line.
3. *Seek acceptance by the outside sales force.* Realize that no one is your enemy. The outside sales force may, at first, feel invaded by your activities. Seek your management's support, because you will need to work with them. I believe the outside sales team will eventually come around when they realize you're an asset and not a detriment.
4. *See the change as a great opportunity.* This process offers

you a chance to sell and make more money, as well as achieve greater goals. Not many people these days are presented with opportunities like that.

5. *Have fun.* Remember that this process is a stepping-stone to greater advancement and security at your company. That, too, is a major factor in your favor.

6. *Pretend your goal is getting to the Carnegie Hall version of selling.* Now, I believe if you head toward Broadway . . .

Index

ACSRs, *see* advanced consultative service representatives
action steps, 69–79
  and closing the sale, 196–198
  and dialogue-probing questions, 75–79
  examples of, 70–72
  identifying, 69–70
  prioritizing with, 73–74
  questionnaires with, 71, 72, 75
advanced consultative selling skills, 1, 20
advanced consultative service representatives (ACSRs), 4, 6, 18, 134
advantages, 144
agenda, setting the, 51
The American Family (Dan Quayle), 113–114

bank tellers, 3
benefit/feature selling, 141–146
benefit summary, 138–139
body language, 37
bridging, 34–35, 42–45
  with funnels, 103–104
  with MLPQs, 81
Burton, Bob
  on offering other products to customers, 20

on reorganization of customer service, 15–16
buyer focus, maintaining, 176–177
buying signals, 33, 184–185, 198–202

"champions," 121–122
change, 10–11
  in customer relationships, 19–20
  and overcoming customer resistance, 172–173
  response of CSRs to, 14–18
  uncovering customer's need for, 96
closing the sale, 181–204
  and customer list items, 187–189
  and customer service, 202–203
  key occurrences as element of, 185–187
  and picking up on buying signals, 184–185
  and recognizing buying signals, 198–202
  and sales cycle design, 189–198
  as step in sales process, 182–183